"A book to savor... take your time w
the continuum, from those intern;
joy. She lets us into places very few
Nancy Ortberg, author of *Seeing in the Dark: Finding God's Light in the Most Unexpected Places*

"*A Good Way Through* is for the wanderer, the seeker, the daughter or son who desires healing but doubts the first steps to take. Here is the guide. Kristen's wisdom and vulnerability will leave you breathless and inspired—hungry to pursue God in new and beautiful and life-changing ways."
Jennifer J. Camp, author of *Breathing Eden: Conversations with God on Light, Fresh Air, and New Things*

"Kristen Kludt pulled it off. She has written a book that is at once wise, intimate, and brave, while also being beautifully crafted. There is an endless supply of books to read, but there are precious few books that feel like they are reading me. *A Good Way Through* is one of them. With each page I felt like I was being gently invited to follow Kludt's lead, to become more present to the one precious life I've been given, and to journey into the unknown with courage and vulnerability and hope."
John Pattison, co-author of *Slow Church: Cultivating Community in the Patient Way of Jesus*

"Kristen's courage is evidenced in her vulnerability about friendship, community life, and infertility, amongst others of life's struggles. Like a true friend, Kristen shares not only spiritual practices that have been life-giving to her, but also her wounds in a way which allows her readers to find healing and hope."
A.J. Swoboda, PhD, professor, pastor, author of *The Dusty Ones*

"From my first read of the manuscript that became *A Good Way Through,* I knew I was encountering something special: a work whose sincere faith was not opposed to its honesty; whose beauty complemented its depth of truth. Privileged as I am to have worked with Kristen to develop her manuscript, I know this work better than most—and I am convinced that it rests in that special literary category of books that cannot merely be read, but must be wrestled, felt, and lived. God, it is said, rewards those who diligently seek him. In this book, Kristen has shared her reward with the world. How immensely generous. For that kindness, we should each be deeply grateful—and allow her wisdom to encourage our own journeys into hope."
Paul J. Pastor, author of *The Face of the Deep: exploring the mysterious person of the Holy Spirit*

"*A Good Way Through* uses story to invite us to a new imagination of a partnership with God, encouraging us to participate in his healing in our lives. Kristen's practices, offered throughout, invite whole-person investigation, drawing us into the kind of learning that finds itself at home in our lives. This deeply-lived, beautifully written book will prove a generous friend for the journey towards hope and healing."
Mandy Smith, pastor, author of *The Vulnerable Pastor: How Human Limitations Empower Our Ministries*

"Being critical and assigning blame, particularly in the shadow of struggle, pain and crisis, are the easiest things to do. What is harder and far better is to ask what can be made of the elements and moments we are given, regardless of their darkness or light. Asking those questions and following them to their actionable end is what artists do. Kristen Kludt is an artist."
Justin McRoberts, author, songwriter

"Kristen Kludt is courageously offering her readers a glimpse into her experience of a reality of life too many of us seek to avoid. In this book she doesn't demand you to embrace or even follow her path toward healing, rather she simply reveals her journey with pain, suffering, and disappointment honestly, which feels like a kind invitation to hold your own journey with wonder, curiosity, and hope."
Dwight J. Friesen, Associate Professor of Practical Theology, *The Seattle School of Theology & Psychology;* co-author of *The New Parish* and *Routes and Radishes*; author of *Thy Kingdom Connected*

"Yes, the writing is exquisite. Yes, the imaginative weaving back and forth across the drama reels you in. But, is it possible for such bleeding poetry, intimate storytelling, and soulful metaphor to be practical? Applicable? Transformative even? Kristen Kludt understands what a rare few writers know—that in her most particular and personal stories, *you* are going to see *you*! And when you do, you will be grateful to have an experienced guide."
Paul Sparks, co-founder of the Parish Collective, co-author of *The New Parish*

"When our soul shivers in the dead of winter, feeling isolated and alone, we need a companion to guide us. Kristen Kludt grabs our hand and takes us on a journey through her disappointments and despair in order to show us *A Good Way Through*. This book will help you develop hope that spring is on the way!"
JR Woodward, National Director of V3 Church Planting Movement, author of *Creating A Missional Culture* and The Church as Movement

"Reading *A Good Way Through* felt like someone was peering into my soul and putting into words emotions and longings that have never been articulated. This book will be a breath of fresh air for anyone looking for hope and understanding in the midst of disappointment, questions, and struggle. And for those who aren't currently walking through a trial, the tools you find here are ones you will want to tuck away for any dark days. These words are a ray of sunlight and a welcome companion in every season."
Elizabeth Hunnicutt, singer-songwriter; worship pastor, Twin Lakes Church

"Kristen offers a much needed feminine voice to the darker side of being human. With a humility seasoned by real life, she explores the complexities of pain, doubt, fear, disappointment, and uncertainty but doesn't leave us there. Instead, her gift as a spiritual guide paired with her commitment to a practiced life empower us beyond the muck and into new-found freedom and formation as God's beloved."
Jer Swigart, Co-Founding Director, The Global Immersion Project

"As our world continues to rumble with opportunities for disembodiment, numbing and masking of our true selves, Kristen invites her readers to an alternative path of authenticity and wholeness. Offering guided practices, enchanting poetry and her vulnerable stories of friendship, bravery, mourning and motherhood, Kristen's book connects with the heart of all of us and restores our hope for God's light in darkness."
Christiana Rice, Missional Leadership Coach and Trainer, Thresholds; co-author of *To Alter Your World: Partnering with God to Rebirth Our Communities*

"None of us can avoid facing seasons of pain. When such a season comes calling, we have a choice to make: Will we be swallowed under—or rather, will we let our pain transform us in ways that leave us better than we were before? Kristen Kludt has chosen the latter in *A Good Way Through*. And Kristen goes a step further by sharing the unique spiritual practices that helped her find her way. We need not wait for tragedy to strike before allowing our big and small losses to transform us. We can begin today—and reading this touching, personal, practical memoir is a great way to start."
September Vaudrey, author of *Colors of Goodbye: A Memoir of Holding On, Letting Go, and Reclaiming Joy in the Wake of Loss*

"In *A Good Way Through*, Kristen stirs my soul to allow my time with the Lord to be a genuine outflow of my actual life; she spurs me on to not want to waste the precious time I do have, but to use it well, deeply, and wisely. This book is a gem, just like the heart from which it springs. Drink deeply."
Stephanie Seefeldt, worship leader; music director, Zion Episcopal Church

A GOOD

way

THROUGH

To Susan —

Many Blessings along the Way!

Kristy Leigh Paulette

A GOOD
way
THROUGH

My Journey with God from
Disappointment into Hope

Kristen Leigh Kludt

Scriptures taken from the Holy Bible, New International Version®,
NIV®. Copyright © 1973, 1978, 1984, 2011 by Biblica, Inc.™
Used by permission of Zondervan.
All rights reserved worldwide. www.zondervan.com The "NIV"
and "New International Version" are trademarks registered in
the United States Patent and Trademark Office by Biblica, Inc.™

Editor: Paul J. Pastor
Cover Design: Ryan Littrell
Interior Design: Rick Szuecs
Copyeditor: Proof Positive Papers
Author Photo: Heidi Ameli

ISBN: 978-1-5370-6806-0
Library of Congress Control Number: 2016916915
CreateSpace Independent Publishing Platform,
North Charleston, SC

*We shall not cease from exploration
And the end of all our exploring
Will be to arrive where we started
And know the place for the first time.*

— T. S. Eliot, *Little Gidding*

For Everett Wendell and Asher Linden—
May you know deep in your bones that you are God's beloved,
and may your lives flow from that knowledge.

CONTENTS

FOREWORD

JUNE OF 1990 was radiant. That summer we walked hand-in-hand dreaming about the life we would make together. We were drunk on our love and youth. The Berlin Wall had just come down, and the Cold War was finally over. As a dramatic backdrop to our story, Russian president Mikael Gorbachev was visiting Minnesota, our home state, on the day we got engaged. Family and friends celebrated our potential, and we had enough good grades and relative privilege to believe that anything was possible. We were going to change the world!

In the fall, both of us were hired to direct programs at a well-respected, faith-based community-development agency in Minneapolis that served at-risk children and families. How fortunate to be fresh out of college doing something we loved! But quickly our dream jobs turned into a nightmare. We discovered that the executive director was physically assaulting the young children in our programs and often verbally accosted our adult clients. When Mark confronted her, our employer literally beat him to the floor. In December, Lisa's parents helped us make the difficult decision to leave our positions. The next two months we were jobless and depressed. Our hopes and ideals lay shattered on the frozen ground we walked that winter. This wasn't how life was supposed to be. What had we done to deserve such misfortune?

By spring, we had found other work and were busy making plans for our summer wedding. The joy and fun of our first year of marriage were tempered by the trauma of the previous autumn. There were smiles on our faces, but anyone who got close enough could see that our wounds were still bleeding. We leaked disappointment onto anyone who would listen.

Ready to put a hard year behind us, we spent the holidays with our families in New York and Minnesota. On January 2, Lisa went to the mall to shop with her father. Leaving him in the food court, she returned as he collapsed on the floor surrounded by onlookers. He was dead. His heart had failed, and we were heartbroken. The coming months introduced us to a level of grief we hardly knew existed and exposed many of our unhealthy patterns for dealing with sadness and stress.

Life was proving to be more difficult and complicated than we had ever imagined—and there would be more: a miscarriage, financial setbacks, health scares, job failures, relational conflicts, and episodes of depression. Of course, we've also had our share of joys, successes, and fun times to celebrate. But for a long time, we suffered from ideas about God, ourselves, and how life works that did not adequately account for the breadth of our real-world experiences. Our responses often revealed false self-messages we had unwittingly believed and rehearsed. Life no longer worked, and we found ourselves in search of a good way through.

Thankfully, along the way, we stumbled onto many of the helpful perspectives and practices Kristen Kludt conveys through her story.

What we learned on our own journey of healing has profoundly shaped the direction of our work. We've spent the past 18 years creating resources and facilitating experiences to help people apply spiritual wisdom to everyday life. We've had the opportunity to walk with many people through critical stages of adulthood and discovered that our experiences of disappointment and difficulty are not uncommon.

At some point, most of us will be bamboozled by life. If it hasn't happened to you yet, it will. Suffering is a necessary and inevitable part of the human journey. Our sense of satisfaction is largely determined by how we learn to navigate seasons of disappointment, failure, loneliness, and pain. If we have the courage to face the hard things, they have much to teach us. Crisis often awakens us to the invitation to grow and change.

We couldn't help but be slightly jealous of the freedom with which Kristen expresses herself. When we were coming of age, spiritual authors didn't write with such honesty and candor about negative emotions or bodily fluids. With this book, Kristen Kludt has given us the gift of her vulnerability. She has shown courage by carefully reflecting on the difficult surprises in her life. Whether your challenges are similar to or different from hers, in these pages you'll discover a way of seeing and practices that can help you find a good way through.

We met Kristen one spring day in Seattle. She and her husband Dave invited us to lunch to talk about their hopes and dreams as a family. We were immediately captured by their playfulness, joy, and intentionality. These were kindred spirits, and we became fast friends. A few months later, we had a chance to walk the streets of Kristen's East Hollywood neighborhood with her. We followed her from Thai market to coffee shop to taco stand, and she seemed to know everyone, greeting them warmly. It's evident that Kristen deeply values relationships.

Kristen's story illustrates that one key to a good way through is supportive friendships. Along the path, she found friends and mentors who could listen, love, and laugh with her. Facing disappointment can be lonely and isolating. A common tendency is to try to navigate pain privately and feel cut off from our communities when we need their support the most. On the flip side, as we witness those we love going through difficulty, it is hard to know how to respond. Our best words can seem trite and hollow.

We need people who can care for us well. But when you feel needy, it can be hard to reach out with confidence. If you don't feel like you have adequate support for what you are going through right now, keep asking and looking. The companionship you need may come from an unlikely source. Most people would be honored if you asked them to be a mentor or support.

Kristen shows wisdom beyond her years. Some of this may be attributed to the risk she has taken to practice silence, solitude, and self-reflection. Contemplative space has been an integral part of her journey of healing and wholeness. Making room to be alone can be difficult in an age of constant distractions and ready escapes. It can be scary to face the flood of thoughts and feelings that reveal themselves in silence. But creating space can help you become more self-aware and experience the Creator's caring presence more fully.

When we visit Kristen's house, we are impressed by the amount artwork displayed on the walls in almost every room— drawings and paintings she has made herself. With purpose, she has experimented with creative practices that have helped her embrace the beauty and particularities of her own story. As you will see, art-making has been an important part of Kristen's journey. We've also found art making to be a powerful integrative tool for healing. Humans have always made things to explore and express the beauty and terror of life. Art-making helps us appreciate the small wonders and connect our experiences to a more cohesive larger narrative. Whether or not you think of yourself as an "artist," the creative practices in this book can help you value and make sense of your experiences. Let Kristen's example inspire you to create your own poems, laments, and artifacts.

Kristen draws on her expertise as an educator and experienced group facilitator. While this book is written as a story, is has much to teach. Kristen has left bread crumbs along the way to introduce you to practices that may help you find a good way through.

Paula D'Arcy famously said, "God comes to you disguised as your life." Scripture suggests that "the Lord is close to the brokenhearted" and that those who mourn are blessed, "for they will be comforted." The divine parent meets us in our pain, recognizes our distress, and compassionately walks with us through it.

May you discover the freedom and courage to meet God, yourself, and others in all the seasons of your life. If it's fall or winter now, spring and summer are still coming.

Mark and Lisa Scandrette

Cofounders of ReIMAGINE: A Center For Integral Christian Practice and authors of *Belonging and Becoming* and *FREE: Spending Your Time and Money on What Matters Most.*

September 26, 2016
San Francisco, California

CAMBODIA: A BEGINNING

THE FALL

Walking in the woods the other day
I came upon a tree lying prone
It was dizzying, disorienting—
this giant, once reaching toward the sky
now reaching sideways,
its green leaves yet unaware
of the death creeping up its roots.
Where it fell there is a hole in the sky.

TRAGICALLY beautiful.

Again and again, my husband and I spoke those words to each other as we traveled through Cambodia in search of adventure and a broadening of ourselves and our understanding of the world. Cambodia's people, her land, and her stories were utterly beautiful, but open wounds of tragedy were everywhere: poverty, violence, sex-trafficking, slavery, and genocide. The violence is fresh. We wandered among the bones of the massacred in the Killing Fields and through the halls of the prison and torture chamber called S-21. We saw photos of the condemned and the killers. We walked dirt streets and rode busses with their friends and with their children.

Yet, Cambodia's beauty is breathtaking. We climbed to the tops of ancient temples and slept in a tree house overlooking the islands of Vietnam. Former street children received vocational training as chefs and servers at our favorite restaurants. We heard stories of hope—of peacemaking and education and growing cross-cultural friendships.

Somehow, beauty and tragedy each make the other more poignant.

We took a bus to Siem Reap, land of the ancient temples. The bus was crowded; people filled the aisle perched on colorful child-sized plastic chairs. The two year old across the aisle from us snacked on a bag of crickets, pulling the legs off one by one and dropping them on the floor. Khmer karaoke and comedy sketches played on the TV screen at the front of the bus. At one point, a Khmer comedian broke suddenly from his monologue and exclaimed, in clear English, "James Bond, American spy!" The bus echoed in laughter, heads turning toward us, smiling. We smiled silently back.

One day, we rented bikes. Bicycles were the perfect way to see the temples: slow enough to take in the surroundings, fast enough to complete a small loop in a day, and independent—we wouldn't have a driver waiting for us. The only downside was that Dave, at six-foot-three, is taller than the average tourist, and his knees jostled his elbows at every rotation of the pedals.

The most memorable of the temples was Ta Prohm, the temple of Tomb Raider fame. Most of the temples have been meticulously restored—invading trees and plants have been torn out and held at bay, tumbled-down, earth-covered rocks have been excavated and restored to their original locations, even stone carvings have been repaired or replicated to recreate the temples in their original glory. Ta Prohm is the exception. There, nature reigns, carving out passageways among the rocks, tumbling stones into piles of rubble complete with the faces of dying gods. The roots of the Banyan trees branch out over the walls, flowing like river deltas into the earth. We walked among cascades of rock, root, and branch, watching butterflies dance in green-hued patches of sunlight.

Soon, this temple would mirror my own heart.

Cambodia was our final adventure before we started trying to have children. We were ready the spring before our trip, but waited because malaria medicine can be dangerous during pregnancy. We would wait until our return home in August. The birth would be perfectly timed for the start of the following spring break, so I could take leave from my teaching job for the rest of the school year and have the summer off. This was the next step in building the beautiful, meticulously crafted temple I called life.

Up until this point, my life had more or less followed the plans I had laid. I was blessed. In fact, sometimes I feared life was too good and disaster must be secretly advancing. I had a wonderful family and grew up in the best neighborhood in the best city for raising kids in the country, which made us the best family in the world, as we always used to say. My parents reminded my sister and me often to be thankful for these good things—not everyone gets to live this sort of life. I was raised in a community of Christians who loved me well and showed me a faith that carried me and still does. My faith grows and transforms as I do. I married my best friend right out of college, and although I moved to a city I was not excited about, I began what turned into a love story with Los Angeles—an arranged marriage of sorts. I found my dream job teaching seventh-grade English at an excellent school just a couple of miles from our new apartment. We had challenges as newlyweds, paying for graduate school on a new teacher's salary—our apartment was mostly a hallway, so narrow you couldn't open the refrigerator door all the way because it collided with the wall—but, for the most part, life continued to unfold better than I could have imagined. We made dear friends at the graduate school, we found a church community that shaped our lives and selves much more than we thought a church could, and we settled into married life with relative ease.

Somewhere along the line, though things were working out quite beautifully in many ways, my meticulously built temple-of-a-life began to crack. I was far from home and my family, who were also my best friends. I had a few difficult moments with close friends in Los Angeles that left me wondering if I was worth befriending. Sometimes I was overwhelmed with emotions I couldn't explain. Dave mentioned therapy. Rocks in my temple began to tumble.

Then there was infertility. Typing that word sends shudders up my fingers through my arms and into my chest—shudders at the pain it brought to me, and at the pain it still is for some of those who are dearest to me. It is an ugly word.

The walls of my temple crumbled. There was no denying that my carefully-constructed world was falling to pieces, exposing raw, hurting parts of my deepest self that balked at the piercing daylight. Who was I becoming?

There is beauty in destruction. The trees of Ta Prohm break apart the rock, filling it with tumbling, growing, moving, death-defying life, making it the most alluring of all the temples in Cambodia. Everywhere else, that life is beaten back to preserve the lovely status quo, the restored monuments of history in rock. Yet, the most spiritual of temples seems to me, and to many, to be the temple that is slowly dying, giving way to the flow of green.

We left Ta Prohm in the mid-afternoon sunshine, heading toward the largest of the temples: Angkor Wat, the iconic temple of the ancient Khmer people, displayed proudly on the Cambodian flag. We climbed its towers and roamed its walls, surveying the vast landscape from above and following the histories carved into the walls below.

As we wandered the field before the temple, gray clouds gathered, turning the late-afternoon light a rusty orange. Then suddenly the sky cracked open and drenched the earth in a torrent of rain. Never had I seen so much water.

We ran to a stone guardhouse to shelter from the rain. Water bounced and echoed off the rock, springing every which way in a merry dance, bringing new life. I sat in a windowpane, back against the cool stone. Others were there, too—a strange mix of tourists and Khmer, young people and old people, laughing together in amazement at this sudden cleansing of earth and stone, man, woman, and sky. I held my hand out, cupping my fingers to catch a little puddle of the cascade. The rain cooled me. Time stopped as we—earth and sky, woman and man—were washed clean.

As suddenly as the clouds had broken open, they knit back together into a dark blanket and drifted away. They left in their wake a brilliant rainbow, shimmering in an enormous arc over the wet, gray walls of the temple. All of us caught our breath in awe, then ran out into the bejeweled grass.

I wanted to linger in that moment, in the magic of it—strangers joined together in a joyful dance of gratitude for rain, for storm, for the violent thunder that brings new life and shimmering color to us and to the earth. But we had bikes to return to, and a ride home in the dark.

We wiped our seats off with a krama—the all-purpose Cambodian scarf, from towel to hammock to diaper—and biked home as dusk fell. As we left the temples behind, we heard the patter of bare feet running beside us. Dave was in front of me, biking slowly. "Hi!" said one boy, about eight years old. He was running with a friend who carried an enormous bag of empty cans. Ahead of them, running alongside Dave, was a little boy of about five.

I called to Dave, "Careful, honey! He's climbing on!" With the agility of a practiced athlete, the tiny boy launched himself onto the bike, clinging to Dave's backpack, feet resting on the chain stay.

Soon, I had a request: "Can I ride?" one of my quickly running new friends asked.

"OK!" I replied. "Careful!" An unnecessary caution.

We biked slowly, trying not to leave the can-carrying pedestrian behind. Dave's little passenger chattered away in Khmer, occasionally throwing out a word or two in English.

"What do we do?" asked Dave.

"I don't know!" I yelled back over the chattering kids and the hum of the bikes. "I guess they know what they're doing! We're probably giving them a ride home!"

We hummed along in the dark to the chatter of voices and the patter of feet on pavement. Occasionally, the clash and clang of cans shifting shoulder-to-shoulder in a plastic bag punctuated our song.

Nearly a mile later, now in the pitch black, still wet from rain, Dave felt a tug on his T-shirt. A tiny hand pointed, and Dave stopped the bike. Our stowaways jumped down and ran across the paved road to a gravel one. The littlest boy paused before running away home. He turned, pressed his palms together, then gave a tiny bow. A quick wave and a grin and he ran off after the others, up the road, to a home in the dark.

The faith and gratitude of children: That is why this moment will forever be imprinted in my mind. There is something about those children—their running feet, their confidence in that spring from wet earth to moving bicycle, their faith in a stranger to bring them home. There is much to grieve and to fear for them, making their own way in an unpredictable world, but there is also much to learn from them. I, too, must learn to jump, to spring from safe ground to moving, spinning, bicycle, to hold on as best I can and trust where it is going.

In the old days, I would rather have kept my feet firmly planted, frantically pulling weeds from the walls of my temple, begging them not to collapse. Now, I am learning the beauty that comes out of destruction, the fresh life that grows clean after a storm, and the exhilaration and joy that go hand-in-hand with the fear of taking a flying leap.

This is a story of healing. I began in a place of fear and doubt, of believing, though I didn't know it then, that God was angry and I was not good enough. In losing myself, I began to find... what, exactly? Grace. Trust. Hope. Joy. Through art and creativity, through deep and abiding friendships, and through the beauty of this world, I met God in the dark places. I found God in the destruction and in the storm and on frightening, unknown roads. Now, by a miracle I am just beginning to understand, I believe God loves me and God is near.

This book is, first, the story of my participation in God's healing in my life. Second, it is a guide to help you discover your own practices for healing.

There is no way to avoid hard things, but there is a good way through them. When we relentlessly open ourselves to God's love, we are transformed, even in darkness.

My friend Justin McRoberts pointed out to me recently that Jesus, when he healed people, almost always asked them to *do* something. The task itself often seemed either random or impossible: "Go wash yourself in the river," or "Pick up your mat and walk." The point, perhaps, is this: We are invited to participate in our own healing. Healing, I am learning, is a choice.

When I experienced depression, my habits of reading my Bible, praying as I had always prayed, and writing in my journal didn't leave me feeling connected with God the way I hoped they would. When I explored new practices along with the old ones, I experienced God's healing presence in new ways. As I entered the darkness within, I discovered that God met me there in art, poetry, friendship, and the natural world. My old habits remained, but they became more meaningful as I engaged new practices alongside them. Much of my journaling turned into poetry, which you will see at the start of each chapter; these are the poems I wrote in this season of darkness as I sought God and transformation.

My hope, as you read this book, is that you will discover your own practices that open you to God's love and transforming power. For me, it was art and poetry. For you, it might be woodworking or running, or whatever restores you. As you read:

- First, immerse yourself in the story.
- As you finish each section, try one or two of the practices. Come back to others when the time feels right.
- If you can, read this book with someone else, someone with whom you can discuss your experience of the practices. We have a lot to learn from each other.

These practices are not meant to be a linear journey but touchstones to return to as the seasons of your life change. The practices themselves will not transform you; only God can do that. They are simply how I made room for God's Spirit to work. My hope is that through this book, you will discover your own ways of making room.

I am no expert in hardship. This book will not fix a hard situation, nor is it a roadmap into God's presence. It is my story of healing and what wisdom came out of it.

We all experience darkness. I offer you mine in the hope that you might find within it light to guide you in your own. May God hold you on your journey, as I know God will.

I. BELOVED IN DISAPPOINTMENT

Let the morning bring me word of your unfailing love,
for I have put my trust in you.
Psalm 143:8

THE GRAND EXPERIMENT

WAIT

We

in our beginning
all hope and eagerness embarked
in the early hours of July.
The story then was much the same
alone, but not alone, I laugh with you.
Their home then our home now Our home
and you are my constant.
Your ocean eyes—
their ebb and flow follow the burst of sun
that shines upon their waters.
I commit to you
my life to your life
my body to your body
my soul to your soul.
Sitting on the porches of our tomorrows
I wonder with you.
(A finger traces the edge of a tablecloth
and bare toes scuff at the aging floor.)
When will the screen door creak
and open
and let us in?
And who will be waiting?
I will wait with you
in the early hours
in the breezy afternoon
when dusk falls on this place.

IN JUNE OF 2009, Dave and I moved fourteen miles from Pasadena to East Hollywood, and from an apartment of our own to a house with two friends from our church, Kairos. Dave was finishing up graduate school, and we had decided to continue our life in Los Angeles a little bit longer. Dave loved the city, I loved my teaching job, and we both loved

Kairos, so we agreed to one more year in Los Angeles. Our two new housemates, Ryan and Peter, were looking for a more intentional rhythm of life with a small family of people; Dave and I hoped to move closer to Kairos and longed for the same.

It had taken several months of conversation for me to feel ready to say "yes" to living in community with people. It excited Dave, but I was afraid of how living with someone else would affect our family of two, and eventually (I hoped) three or four. Dave and I talked about what it would look like, then invited Ryan and Peter into the conversation. We dreamed of regular dinners together, connections with neighbors, and the ability to be a home for our church. We talked about finances and cleanliness and how we would find time alone. We talked about accountability and conflict and our hopes for being family for one another, a group of transplants far from home.

We walked the streets of the East Hollywood neighborhood around Kairos together, calling numbers on "For Rent" signs. One night, we walked by a little house on Kenmore Avenue, just two blocks from the building where Kairos meets. There was a sign out front with a phone number, and we called. While we set up a time to meet the owners, I looked at the walkway lined with roses, the fruit trees, and the little front porch, and imagined.

I'm a dreamer, but I dream best with the stage set. I have a hard time imagining a future in a new place, and a much easier time imagining a future when I'm looking at the place—when I can see how we might grow there and how the place itself might grow and change with us. My dreams of a familial life in an intentional community became vivid when I saw the house with the stained glass window and the grass in the front yard and imagined conversations sitting on the cracked front steps.

The next day, we visited the house together, walked through the empty living room, and talked about how this place might work. We walked through the backyard, admiring the little house in back, already rented to a friendly couple.

Standing inside of that house, I realized something: *I can do this. I can share this house with these people, and it will be OK.* We put in an application together. The next day, our application was accepted. We had a home.

A year earlier, had you told me we'd be sharing a house with two single men from our church the next summer, I would have thought you had the wrong Krissy. I like my space. I don't like other people's clutter, and I don't like other people being annoyed with my clutter. Whenever we travel, Dave wants to share a suitcase. I always refuse—I have my system, and I don't want someone else's underwear to screw that up. I like having our own fridge and not worrying about other people using metal utensils on our nonstick pans. I like to be in control of when I want to be hospitable. What convinced me to live in community was the realization that those were things about myself I wanted to change. I *wanted* to become more generous, more hospitable, and less protective of my material belongings. I wanted to let go. What better way to do that than to share a home?

Living in intentional community helped our home become a second home for our Kairos family. We hosted a dinner once a week for several years, and everyone knew where to find what they needed when it was their turn to cook. One friend kept a pair of her slippers by our front door. Another friend popped over for a nap between two meetings in our neighborhood. He met his wife in our dining room. I became accustomed to a full house, to lots of extra mouths for our would-be leftovers.

I hoped the four of us would become an adopted family for one another. All of Dave's and my extended family lived in Wisconsin, so I wanted to expand and strengthen our fabric of support in California. I had high expectations for what this community could offer. I didn't know yet that I would soon face the darkest challenges of my adult life.

We wove our lives together in small ways. Once a week we had "snack time," when we checked in on how each of us was doing. All of us were in periods of transition, in a holding pattern of sorts as we figured out what was next in life. We listened to each other, held each other's stories and offered prayer, support, and occasional advice.

There were hard things about community living, especially as a married couple. Once a month, Dave and I kicked everyone out of the house so we could order Thai food and snuggle on the couch in our pajamas and watch movies, an attempt to reclaim the coziness of a house of our own for just one evening. We all had different ideas about how often we should use the heater or how loud it was appropriate to whistle while someone else was trying to read. We had some arguments that recycled over and over, and some that didn't but should have. People came late to house dinners or forgot about them. I had high expectations for what this "family" would become. Like much of life, it never did look exactly as I had imagined, but living in community shaped me and changed me. I did become more hospitable, more flexible, and less possessive. I found new kinds of grace to extend and accept.

In choosing life in an intentional community, I stumbled onto a way of living that has become a marker—the marker, perhaps—of my spiritual life: If you want to be transformed, act. I wanted to become more hospitable, and I could have read about hospitality and talked about hospitality and thought about hospitality, but none of those things would have changed me if I hadn't practiced hospitality.

A little bit of action and a lot of trust and prayer—together, these transform us. You are not responsible for your own transformation. You don't have to will yourself to be better, stronger, or happier. Just take one tiny step in the direction of love. God is the one who heals and transforms us, but we get to participate. We get to choose whether or not to open ourselves to healing.

I didn't know then how hard that was about to become.

WHAT (MY) DEPRESSION IS LIKE

REFLECTION

I sit in the window
as dawn begins to peek around the corner
and morning traffic flows by.
Its edges ripple through the door——
parents and children on their way to school,
businessmen with their briefcases,
the man who sits in the tall chair
wearing a few more layers than the weather merits.
But my back is to them
as I face the window,
the screen of my laptop
brightly lit with this morning's prayer:
"Let my soul rise up to meet you
as the day rises to meet the sun."
And I think about that
as I watch the sun
and I think to myself,
is it really the day who does the rising?
As I sit, and ponder, and pray
those words shuffle through my mind
and I hold my mug of tea
with both hands.
And then
the screen
goes black.
I am struck by the starkness of my own image
lit by the rising sun
against the emptiness behind.
What is it that I see?
I watch her for a moment—
the woman looking back at me——
but only for a moment
before I
tap the mouse
to get back the brightness of this morning's prayer
and forget myself
alone
against the black.

THE DAY WAS BEAUTIFUL. We sat at a picnic table in the shade of a eucalyptus tree hung with yellow balloons. We ate and laughed and ran around the park with the kids.

It was a birthday party, with our birthday-party friends. I can't remember whose birthday it was, only that someone had made mint brownies. We were with friends from our graduate school years. When we'd met five years earlier, we had all recently married and transplanted to Pasadena. We walked through the first two years of school together, running up the street to each other's apartments for a casual dinner or meeting on campus for coffee and a game of cards. One year, we could see into Katie and Joey's apartment from our bedroom window. We would peer out to see if they were home before popping over.

Much had changed in the years since those early days. We had all grown up a bit. Everyone but us had started a family, as we had also intended. Since Dave and I had moved to East Hollywood, we had lost the frequent contact we used to enjoy. Now, for the most part, we saw each other only on birthdays.

Leah Beth and David had two children, Becca and Andrew another two, Katie and Joey had one and another on the way. Our arms were empty.

Dave and I met our freshman year of college. I was dating someone else, and a friend of mine "liked" Dave, so he was off-limits anyway. He and I became good friends and worked closely together, co-leading in our church's college ministry. Our mutual attraction began suddenly two years later. When we finally started dating mid-way through our junior year, our relationship escalated quickly. Two weeks into our dating relationship, I told my mom he was the man I would marry.

Naturally, then, we talked early on about family. We both wanted two kids. We wanted to wait a few years, get Dave through graduate school, and take some time to travel together, but then we would be ready for our family to grow.

Life went as planned for a while. We married just after graduation, then moved to California for Dave's graduate school. We explored near and far in our early years together. Life chugged along as expected, but when it was time to have kids, it came to a dead stop. As each month passed, our realization deepened that this might not be as simple as we'd thought.

While we were trying to get pregnant, reminders of our barrenness were everywhere. It was like when we bought our Prius—suddenly everyone, everywhere owned a Prius. I counted fifteen Priuses one morning between our house and the freeway. The same was true with pregnancy, except instead of being part of the trend, I saw reminders everywhere of what I lacked. Pregnancy was very fashionable that year. Celebrities were becoming pregnant left and right, posing nude on the covers of magazines. Adorable, hip little babies in skinny jeans and flannel infested East Hollywood. All the while, my womb was empty.

In our everyday circle of friends, however, we were fairly safe. Kairos was tiny, and consisted of mostly single and young married "industry" folk—people who, in pursuit of their art, had set aside the idea of kids for a while or forever. That's why I didn't see this coming.

The sun was too hot, the park too full, the perfect foil for my empty womb. I followed little Eli around the playground a while, talked half-heartedly about teaching with the moms (what else did I have to talk about?), and finally settled in where I often did in those days—hovering at Dave's elbow, half-listening to the dads talk about theology and church and family and future. That was easier than listening to chatter about baby food and toddler development or—worse—knowing I was the reason such a natural subject was avoided.

An hour or so into the party, I could no longer hover next to Dave. The pain gnawed at my belly, it hurt too much, and it was spilling out. Hiding my tears, I ran to the park bathroom.

The cool concrete structure mirrored my heart much better than the glare of the sun outside. It was empty, quiet. The fluorescent lights were sterile, unflattering, clinical. I liked them that way. I locked myself into a stall, wrapped my arms tight around my chest, and screamed the silent scream of loss. What was wrong with me? Why was my body so broken, so unable to do what I thought God created it to do? I murmured "why" after "why" aloud to the dirty metal walls. The emptiness of my womb burned like fire. I sobbed in that empty bathroom under the sterile lights and let the fire consume me. I surrendered to grief.

Invitation to Practice: The Feelings Closet

How do we make space to experience our emotions?

See p. 176

I remembered the birthday party. I doused the fire, not yet spent, letting the coals continue to ravage my insides. I wiped my eyes, took a deep breath, and headed back into the sunlight with a smile. I did not want to have anything to explain.

Grief in the unknown: It is baffling. How do you grieve the loss of something that never was? I had so much need in that time, so much pain I couldn't contain. Many days, I just didn't want to be the sad one. People were careful around me, and I needed them to be, but their being careful didn't help the pain. My pain was obvious, no matter how I masked it, no matter how high the walls I built around my heart. Even when I smiled, my eyes were glassy, empty. I was ragged, broken, trying to keep it together enough to be appropriate in public, then screaming silently behind closed doors. How else could I function? We have to go on at times like that. There is no choice. So I danced back and forth between grief and pretending. I let out enough pain often enough that it did not consume me completely, and I faked it the rest of the time.

Where was God in all of this? In my heart, God was distant, angry. I assumed God was disappointed with me and maybe didn't love me much. In reality, I was the distant, angry one—distant, often, even from my own emotions. How could the God I loved let this happen to me? Was I just not worthy of having something to love?

———❊———

These questions intensified in our months of infertility, but they were not new to me. I first remember questioning God's love for me in high school.

Behind my childhood home there was a silver maple, five stories high, with branches that wrapped around the house and hugged my room on two sides. Outside my bedroom window was the roof of the downstairs porch, and I used to climb out onto the roof at night, just to sit under my tree, to watch the wind in its branches. I cried, sang, prayed, and dreamed under that tree. In the minutes before a coming storm, I heard the voice of God in that tree, singing anticipation in its branches, silver leaves shimmering in the wind, whipping through the air like my hair on a windy day.

I felt close to God as a child. I prayed a lot and read my Bible. My belief ran deep; faith in Jesus was the ground I walked on. I believed God was good and Jesus died for me to save me from my brokenness. I worked hard to live up to that gift. I was kind to kids who others disliked. I gave 10 percent of my allowance to church. In high school, I met every week with a mentor, and I took summer trips with the youth group. I discovered the power of musical worship in a new way. I loved my God and the life I lived.

When I was a senior in high school, in the month before my first experience of depression, my beautiful silver maple started to split down the middle. It was a windy summer, and I had to sleep downstairs on a mattress in the family room for a few nights before the tree was taken down, in case it fell on the house.

Men came. First, they stripped the tree of its branches. It became a naked, lopsided trunk. Piles of limp silver-leaved limbs littered the yard. My beautiful tree, provider of summer shade, creator of golden drifts to run and play and hide in during autumn, the screen through which I looked down upon the white winter world, was now bare, its majesty lost to a couple of men with a chainsaw.

Then the trunk was gone, just a few stumps left to chop up for firewood. By the next spring, the only sign that my tree had ever existed was a patch of mushrooms that sprouted one dewy morning.

The sky behind my parents' house still doesn't look right to me.

What do we do when our symbols of God-in-this-world are stripped away?

There were other precipitating factors, but the loss of that tree sparked my first spiral downward. I had my first panic attack. I didn't eat well. I wanted my body to mirror what was happening in my heart—to feel sick, lusterless. My mom cared for me well, talking me through my first panic attack and making me rice with butter when I wouldn't eat anything else. She trusted, through what I know now was plenty of fear in her own heart, that I would come out of it, and I did. I made new friends, tried new things, and found God and myself in new ways. I grew up a little.

In adulthood it was harder, more complicated. My mom was now two thousand miles away. From the outside, I looked much the same, but inside something was different. My blood felt metallic, like I was filled with tiny particles that didn't quite belong, and if I concentrated I could taste them on my tongue, like steel. My self-talk turned cruel. *How could you do that? Why did you say that? That was so stupid. Can you imagine what she's thinking right now? You probably just hurt her feelings and made yourself sound like a total jerk. What were you thinking?* I would never speak to another human being in that judgmental, degrading way. In my deepest heart, a part of me believed this was God's voice, and God was angry with me because I wasn't good enough. I didn't try hard enough. I didn't love well enough. I didn't give enough of myself. Now, to add to the list, I was physically broken. There was something wrong with me that wouldn't allow me to have children, and that was my fault. My body didn't work right. And that was my fault.

I had two strategies to escape the self-talk: I napped a lot, and I kept moving, filling my life with people and activity. I hid from the fear of what was happening in my own heart. I could only hide for so long.

Dave was good to me in my depression. He knew he couldn't fix it, and he didn't try (at least not too often). Instead, he gave me space, asked good questions, and loved me well. After a while, he gently encouraged me to find safe ways to unpack what was happening within me. For a time, he was my one solace, and he couldn't carry me forever.

I started therapy. It helped, though it was awkward at first. I wasn't sure what to do, and Dr. L didn't ask a lot of questions, so I just talked a lot and tried not to feel weird. I called her my human journal, because she didn't seem real—she felt two-dimensional, like a book character, because I didn't know much about her other than her name and her title. She was kind, she listened well and made all the right faces at the right times. As she got to know me, she said a few things and asked a few questions. She would say, "Wow, your god sounds really angry and hard to please." I would say, "No, he isn't!" but then I started to realize my god *was* angry, and I was serving a god who I would never profess I believed in. The God I wanted to serve and thought I knew was infinitely more patient and gracious and loving than the one I was serving.

People asked if I was angry with God because of my infertility. I wasn't. That would have been healthier. Instead, I was terrified of God. I was certain *God* was angry with *me*. I forgot the part of the story where God forgave me, even died for me, knowing full well all of my broken, ugly places. I forgot the oft-repeated words, "Fear not." I felt abandoned, unseen, unworthy, and unwanted. I was looking first at myself and then at people around me to figure out who God was. Now I try my best to reverse the order, and look to what I know about God to try to understand myself and other people.

Therapy, most of the time, felt like groping blindly through fog, searching for something, but without knowing what it was, or where it was, or even if there was anything there at all. I feared I might get lost in the looking. Slowly, therapy loosened some things within me. I started to feel movement in my heart, and, in the end, change.

After my first session I brainstormed in my journal ideas for "homework"—what could I do to live differently after realizing some new things about myself? How could I practice a new way of being? My list of ideas was hazy, mostly having to do with trying harder not to try so hard to be so composed all the time, to act and look and be so darned competent and responsible.

It took a few more months before I stumbled into a much better, more concrete practice: field trips. For four months, every Saturday afternoon I went on a field trip. The only rules were that I went by myself and invited God along.

It's hard to describe how hard this was for me. The person I was least at ease with was myself. Perhaps it was not myself, but this projection of God that I had created based on my deepest fears and hurts. In this moment of desperation, I decided that in order to learn to like myself, I was going to have to hang out with myself. In order to be less afraid of God, I would have to be alone with God.

I began tentative and became joyful. I took myself out for tea a few times and brought books or my watercolor paint set. I tried to be kind to myself. I walked in the Huntington Gardens and remembered that I love to be outside under big trees. I started to look forward to these trips. I went to Griffith Park and Barnsdall Park and the Tim Burton exhibit at the Los Angeles County Museum of Art.

Invitation to Practice: Field Trips

How do we enjoy ourselves alone with God?

See p. 178

That was my favorite because of the eyes. Tim Burton's characters always have huge eyes, eyes that make them seem frightened and sad and maybe a little bit ill, and that's how I felt; I saw myself in the eyes of all those crazy characters. I sat on a bench outside of the exhibit and watched a little kid run around and wished again I had a little kid of my own, and I drew a picture in my journal of a tiny, wide-eyed girl, standing on a windy precipice, and in front of her, looking back at her, was a great Eye, big as the world. The girl was I and the eye was God and I didn't know what it meant, but I knew it felt good to create it, to put on paper something beyond words.

Time passed. I came to a place where I could sometimes be happy and I liked myself a little bit. I became less afraid of my own darkness. I didn't exactly hear from God, but the anger I had perceived from God began to dissipate. I started to believe there was something else surrounding me instead.

Maybe it was love.

Discovering my belovedness required two disparate movements. First, there was an inward movement, a deep dive into my own darkness. I needed to be alone with God in my most tender places and discover I was OK. I needed to find a source of joy within my own heart.

Second, was an outward movement toward other people. In reaction to a broken friendship, I had retreated almost completely. I had put walls between my heart and everyone around me except for Dave. His friendship was enough for a little while, but now I needed to find a measured path toward openness and vulnerability. When I experienced my belovedness alone, I could then experience it more deeply with other people. Out of a growing assurance that I was loved, I could let other people in.

HUNGRY

I AM WINTER

I am winter.
I am the bare, black trees
sharp against the softness of the blue-gray sky.
I am the silent snow.
Come.
Cross my white fields,
smell the biting air, the wool of your scarf,
wet with your breath,
as you carefully step across my icy river,
tumbling softly over stones, under snow.
Smell the smoke from my chimney——I invite you in.
Stomp your boots on my front porch;
shed your frosty layers in my entryway.
Do you hear the teapot sing? It sings for you.
Dry your socks at the fire in my living room;
until the stars fall from their inky chambers,
you never have to leave.

PERHAPS THE DEEPEST of all human desires is the longing to be known and accepted. When I imagined becoming a mother, much came with it: a new and exciting responsibility to care for another human being, membership in the de facto mothering club, and a mysteriously intimate relationship with a human being who would rely on Dave and me completely.

For most of my life, I have been a person of few and deep relationships. When I find deep soul-friends, they feel like rare treasures, and I cling to them. In those days of infertility, I expected a few close friendships to carry the weight of my growing depression. Infertility brought Dave and me closer together, but his experience of it was very different from mine. For him, it felt surreal, as did the idea of having a baby. Infertility didn't carry the same weight of brokenness it did for me, perhaps because, most likely, his body was not the problem. Dave and I talked often about what I was feeling, and he comforted me, but I knew that wasn't enough. I had to find others, too, to process this with, particularly other women.

I would have to tread carefully. I expected much of my friends. Once, my expectations were so high that my disappointment destroyed the friendship.

Maria and I met in college, over corn on the cob. In our senior year, we lived down the street from each other, and our future husbands were roommates on the same block.

In spite of our proximity, I didn't get to know Maria well before she and Mike, married two weeks after Dave and I, came to visit us in California. Then, a year later, they moved to Pasadena, and everything changed. They moved in three apartments down from us. We shared everything. We made grocery lists for each other and took turns grocery shopping. We shared a vacation, squeezing all four of us, all of our camping gear, and all of our food for a week into a two-door Honda Civic.

Maria and I took many evening walks, just the two of us, around the graduate school's quiet campus. We fell into a depth of relationship that surprised us both. As the years went by, my needs grew with my depression, and it became too much for our friendship.

I relied on Maria. She asked all the right questions, pulling hopes and pains out of me that I couldn't find without her. I had disassociated myself from my own heart, and she helped me peel back the layers. I never questioned that. There was an intensity to our relationship that drew me in. I needed Maria to hold me together. That job was too much for her.

We realized it suddenly one day, and after much tearful conversation, we took an extended break from our friendship at Maria's request. I was overcome with shame. I hadn't seen that my own neediness was eroding the foundation of our friendship until the ground fell out from under me. Looking back, Maria and I both know it was a mutual mismatch of needs and struggles that brought about this fall, but at the time I thought it was all my fault. I was not worth befriending.

This shame brought up other fears. If I hadn't recognized my own neediness in this intimate friendship, what else was there within me to which I'd been blind? If Maria, this person who knew me better than anyone in the world aside from my family, had seen my soul and walked away, what could there be within me worth loving? I was broken; I wasn't enough; I was unworthy. I was, at the core, unlovable.

In the midst of all of this was a crisis of faith. I never—or almost never—doubted the existence of the God I grew up with, who created me, who died for me to kill death. Now I suspected that God was disappointed in me, angry with me, maybe even repulsed by me.

In spite of the mess—in fact, because of the mess—Maria was exactly the friend I needed in that moment. Our breakup, as painful as it was, acted as the catalyst for my own journey toward health and restoration. I had to fall before I could be picked back up again. I had to be unwound all the way before I could be knit back together. I had to be laid bare, unquestionably, utterly naked before God, before I could believe God looked on me with love.

The loss of Maria's friendship left me exposed. I wanted to be loved and known, but I was terrified of the power that deep knowing gave another person over my emotional well-being. What if I opened myself to someone else and she also walked away? I couldn't face the thought. Friendships felt like a tug-of-war: a few steps forward, then a hasty retreat.

I had always lived transparently, letting other people into every corner of my life and heart, believing that honesty meant full disclosure of all things to all people who asked me questions. Now I realized that these pieces of myself I offered were gifts given in vulnerability, requiring tenderness.

My healing was an inward and outward dance. Before I could know myself as a worthy friend, I had to know myself as a beloved daughter. I had to find the courage

Invitation to Practice: Boundaries

How do we create healthy boundaries while inviting others into our inner lives?

See p. 180

to look within myself, to see whatever it was that Maria saw. I had to come to know my own need.

"Hungry," my therapist called it, comparing my longing to a child inside of me, longing for love, for care, for relational "food." I could feel my inner child trembling, mouth wide like a baby bird. I was ashamed of her. Growing up, it was a cardinal sin to be needy in my family—we are self-sufficient, independent, competent people. Our life was abundant, love bountiful; to need meant admitting that even this perfect family wasn't enough.

Now I was hungry, and I was afraid: What if other people find out that my hunger for love is insatiable? They will see who I really am, and they will run. It has happened before.

So I hid my inner child. I built high walls around her. I did my best to hide her from myself, and from God. I didn't take care of her. I didn't show her grace. I certainly did not love her.

In the midst of this frightening realization about myself, Anna arrived. My friend Anna, who I hadn't spent more than a few consecutive hours with in eight years, came to visit for a week.

Anna and I met in sixth grade chorus. We passed notes back and forth during class in a hot pink notebook. We sang a duet together in the spring concert. We both cared about making the world a better place, even at the age of eleven.

Anna is one of the most passionate people I have ever known. She throws herself into her work, her relationships, her play. She loves with her whole heart.

Since high school, we'd kept in touch sporadically: a two-hour phone call twice a year, the occasional letter, and coffee dates when we were both home in Wisconsin. I'd forgotten how good it was to be with her.

A few days into her visit, Dave said he was glad to see me having fun with her. We went to art museums, visited the Hollywood stars, ate ice cream and cheesecake and cheap, sloppy burritos. I didn't do that then. Aside from Dave, it had been years since I'd had a friend I had fun with. I'd had church friends, coffee-date friends, pour-your-soul-out-and-cry-over-the-puddle friends, but no run-around-town-like-you're-sixteen-again, eat-yourself-sick, belly-laugh friends. Now here was this glorious week. I was overwhelmed by her affection. Since sixth grade, we've ended every note, letter, and email with the words, "I looooooof you!!!" I never realized what a rare, beautiful gift that was until her visit.

The three of us drove ninety miles to Joshua Tree to camp. While Dave hunkered down to read at the top of a rock, Anna and I set off to explore the desert.

The barren beauty of Joshua Tree reminds me of the moon, or maybe Mars. If Mars had trees, they would be Joshua trees. Maybe it will in a few millennia. The landscape is beautiful and harsh, full of life that fights hard to survive. Anna and I wandered on and off the path, often losing it among the dried-out creek beds that snaked through the rocks. We took goofy pictures posing like trees. We skipped through the desert, singing every song we could remember from our high school choir days: "The One-legged Sailor," "Big Sky," "Siyahamba." We sang at the top of our lungs to no one but the moonscape desert and the wide-open sky. To feel so safe, so myself in that place with another person—it set me free.

Then we found the hole in the rock.

The rocks of Joshua Tree are a contradiction of rough and smooth. Their surface is rough to the touch, gravelly, but the formations themselves are smooth from a distance, rounded, like a carton of eggs or a baby's balled-up fist, worn by centuries of wind and water and sand. This particular rock formation, quite large, had one perfect hole in it: a cave the size of a kitchen cupboard, four feet off the ground. It wanted to be entered.

I climbed into the hole, the rock rough against the palms of my hands, and wrapped arms around bent knees to pull my feet inside. I smelled the dry desert earth. There, in the rock, I was safe—protected from sun and wind, warm, sheltered.

In the crazy-desert-moonscape-dry-creek winter of that year, Anna's visit was my hole in the rock. Her warmth sheltered me from my emotions and my own battered heart for a while. Her effusive love chased away my fear. Anna helped me to see that, perhaps, what my hungry inner child needed was love, comfort, and protection; she wouldn't disappear for hiding or waste away to nothing for neglect.

She needed kindness.

———◊———

The loss of my friendship with Maria left me exposed; Anna's friendship left me protected. Both were stumbling steps toward God. Anna's brief visit gave me hope that I would again find friendships that would reveal God's love to me. Maria's friendship taught me to enter those friendships carefully, and not to expect any one person to carry the weight of my need for love.

Friendship might reveal God's love, but it cannot be the only way we find it. If we only move outward, never inward, our experience of God's love will be dependent on our friendships and could break them. The same is true of marriage. Dave is my best friend, but his love isn't enough, and never will be. When two people carry into their relationship the knowledge that they are beloved already, they are free to love each other well, without grasping. We cannot complete each other; we will only damage the love we have if we try.

When Anna left, I watched for signs of friendship, and I took slow, careful steps toward other people. I went on field trips and I sought out new ways of finding God. I continued my inward and outward dance.

FLICKERS

HOPE

I.
Where is joy?
I looked on the mountainside,
and it was there.
I looked under the oak tree,
and it was there.
I looked behind the flower bed,
and where was I?
Trapped—lost—hidden
beneath the folds of hope-turned-hope-less.
The ever-ending never-ending story
of hope found, hope lost
The sadness under, joy behind
which is at the core?
The core is empty
black
cacophony or symphony?
I listen with muffled ears.

II.
The layers of an onion
*   joy under darkness behind*
*   layer after layer*
and what is left when you get to the core?
A thread pulled
*   and how much will unravel?*
Will there be any of me left
*   when the rest of me falls away?*
I'm afraid of what I'll find.
Once upon a time there was a girl
who trapped a butterfly within a cage
and watched it beat its wings till they were dust
because she was afraid to let it go,
unsure what would remain for her to hold,
unsure what would remain for her to love.

WITH ANNA'S DEPARTURE, the darkness of infertility and the loss of my friendship with Maria dominated my world. I needed to dive deeper into what was happening in my heart. But Anna left behind a hope that new friendships would come. I needed to step outward even as I dove inward.

---※---

"How often do you think about it?" Dave asked me one day, holding me to him during one of our many comforting-each-other-in-our-infertility conversations.

"Every time I go to the bathroom."

There are reminders of infertility everywhere, and one of the most tangible is in the bathroom. I went to the bathroom a lot, just to check, especially in the weeks I was expecting my period. *I think I just started it. Oh wait, no, not yet. Am I having cramps? Or did I just eat something weird for breakfast? No period yet. Am I late? Am I pregnant? I'm not pregnant. I can't be pregnant. Don't think you're pregnant. Maybe I should go see if I started my period again—then at least I'll know and I can stop thinking about it. Yeah, I should probably check.*

On it goes. Pregnancy tests. Ovulation tests. Thermometers. It all feels very scientific, but like that one awful experiment in high school physics where I knew the numbers were supposed to tell me one thing, but they definitely didn't, and I couldn't figure out what I was doing wrong.

I had plenty of sex education class as a kid, and I thought I understood the basics of making a baby. Dave had gone to a Christian school where they left it up to the parents, which meant he knew a lot less of the technical information about what exactly was (or wasn't) happening in my body. I asked him to read about it, to learn what fallopian tubes were. I read books, too, learned about basal body temperature and "egg white" (don't ask). Making a baby seems like something that should feel natural, even pleasurable, but when you're struggling with infertility it quickly becomes technical, scientific, and dehumanizing.

For months, I took my temperature first thing every morning and graphed it, hoping to see it spike. It never seemed to spike when it was supposed to, always much later, and then I'd start my period again and know we had missed the window. I bought ovulation test kits, thinking my temperature readings weren't working. If you've never used one before, they're like a pregnancy test—you pee on a stick and it tells you if you're ovulating—but it has to be at just the right time every day and you have to be drinking the right amount of liquid at the right times, and I couldn't seem to get one to work. I have a distinct memory of camping during the key week and trying to figure out how to surreptitiously dispose of said stick after emerging from the bathroom without any of our friends noticing. Then there was the question of what to do if I was ovulating on a camping trip with a group of friends.

I thought about infertility all the time. Dave's question was like asking someone on a sailboat trying to plot their way out of a thunderstorm with a broken GPS, "How often do you think about it?" A more fitting question might be, "How do you ever think about anything else?" At least that's what it felt like for me.

Infertility is consuming and isolating. I am hopeful that this is changing—more people are talking about it and writing about it than even a few years ago—but we felt very alone. As much as Dave was heartbroken with me, it was different for me. Infertility felt more connected to the core of who I was, more confusing and earth-shattering as well as sad. Dave was upset about it, he cried about it, but he didn't think about it all the time like I did. He didn't lose his way in it like I did. This darkness consumed me, but I was becoming less afraid of it.

Then I met Abby.

⸙

In my season of unfolding darkness, Abby was light. Something about her sparkling eyes said, "Trust me." Perhaps it was their eagerness—she was lonely, too. Having recently moved to Los Angeles, she had space in her life for me; she needed a friend, too. I took tentative steps toward her. She met every step with a smile.

We had our first cup of coffee together at Coffee by the Books, sitting at a high table by the wide window. I pressed my palms to my warm mug, and I talked about infertility with her. I told her about the woman I had walked past that morning, pushing several dirty stuffed animals ahead of her in a shopping cart, and how it terrified me that I understood that woman: In her I saw my own instinctual, gut-wrenching desire to care for something, anything. My openness was a risk, and I told Abby so. "I wouldn't usually say this on a first coffee date, but I think we're going to be good friends." I was telling her that this piece of my heart I was giving to her was precious. I was no longer ignorant of my tenderness. I tread carefully.

I was open with Abby, but more profoundly, I had fun with her.

Even as a child, I was serious, intense. I like talking about the transcendent and spending my time on the transformative. I'm not good at frivolity.

Not long after we met, Abby and I took our first "road trip," all the way to her apartment in Pasadena. We snuck into a monastery to take photos together, we painted on

Invitation to Practice: How to Make a Friend

How do we make friends?

See p. 183

her floor, we snuggled into her bed, watched *The Last of the Mohicans* on her laptop and cried. We made no plans, had no agenda—we simply enjoyed each other's presence.

That was the first of many road trips, some local, some less so. Wherever we ended up, our road trips looked much the same: naps, frozen yogurt, art, movies, and time outside under the wide California sky. We made dinners together, crazy concoctions usually involving hummus. In those moments, Abby taught me how to let go.

On every road trip, we got lost at least once, most often between her house and mine. Happily chatting away, we'd miss a turn or an exit and end up going far out of our way. We enjoyed each other's presence so thoroughly that we truly didn't mind. With Abby, I enjoyed life's detours.

A few months into our friendship, I found out our back house neighbors were moving. Just a month later, Abby moved in. For a year and a half, we shared a yard. We lived close enough to pop over to one another's houses every day, sharing pots of tea. That proximity solidified our quickly-growing friendship.

When I first met Abby, I was not yet ready to invite another person into my darkness—that was still a solitary journey. I first had to find peace and joy and grace in the light. Abby is beautiful, fun, wise, adventurous, deep—the kind of person everyone wants to get to know—and she picked me. She chose me to be her friend, even though I had my sad and lonely days. She liked me. In her presence, I liked me, too.

Slowly, as I learned to experience love and joy even in my depression, I became braver about inviting other people into my darkness and about exploring it myself. The only way out was to go deeper in.

Abby and I started a writing group. We only met a handful of times, but the space was sacred. Our first meeting was in Abby's tiny apartment. We curled up on the couch and sprawled on the floor and wrote. We shared little bits of what we'd written and marveled at each other's artistry and honesty. I spilled my soul a little bit and made room for new things to grow. I trusted these women with one small piece of my inner landscape.

Invitation to Practice: Creative Writing

How might we invite God's voice into the processing of our (sometimes incomprehensible) feelings?

See p. 185

The second time the group met, my coworker Stephanie came. She wrote much and said little, just that she had spilled out some of the darkness inside of her. I wanted to know more, to see if her darkness looked like my own.

It did.

Stephanie, who taught eighth-grade English, was several years into her own journey of infertility. She, too, was trying to stumble toward a God she had always known but wasn't sure she understood, especially in the darkness she found herself in.

Stephanie is like a poem.

Poetry unfolds me. It gives me words when I have none. Poems say what cannot be said, define what cannot be defined, and in so doing they open me—to mystery, to questions, to my own heart. Poems, in their attempt to express the inexpressible, reach down inside my soul and lay things open. They shine lights into deep places and help me see. They are neither spotlight nor flashlight, but candlelight. They help me to distinguish what moves in the shadows; in them I glimpse what lurks inside my heart. I was afraid in those days that if I looked too hard at my own soul I would see something beyond redemption. But the light of a poem is safe, its way gentle. Poems let me move cautiously in the shadows, lighting the way just enough.

Stephanie, too, is gentle. Stephanie, too, is safe.

In Stephanie, I found a trusted companion to enter the darkness. The more time I spent with her, the more I understood myself.

Infertility, or any kind of tragedy or unmet longing, splays us open. I was raw, open wide to the world, vulnerable to everything and everyone around me because of my pain. I was open to hard things, but I was also open to good things. That's where poetry came from: The entryway into my soul was open wide, and in that threshold, art came out of me that I didn't know I had the ability to create. Slowly, through creativity and these fledgling friendships, I was beginning to change.

ACORN FAITH

THE GREAT OAK
Standing before the altar,
I raised my eyes to heaven,
unashamed.

There grew, by the place,
an oak with wide-spreading branches.

Then the tree shook—

and night came on.

Dawn, and morning.

The tree stood before me,
still,
her branches blooming,
twigs swirling,
and her flowers were faces.

I heard, "Behold!"

I gazed with wonder,
kneeling.

IN MY EXPERIENCE of Los Angeles, everyone who lives there, regardless of years, seems young. You have to be resilient, creative, and perhaps just a little bit self-focused to survive there. On my first day of teaching, just after we had moved to LA, I noticed trucks unloading equipment in the school soccer field. "What is that?" I asked a colleague.

"The industry," she said, as if that explained everything. In time, I would discover it did. "The industry" in Los Angeles is the entertainment industry, and much of the life of the city revolves around it. The culture is fast-paced, even cutthroat. People hoping to "make it" in LA save up all the money they can, and land there ready to work around the clock to succeed. They sacrifice sleep, comfort, even friendships to try to live into their calling. A few succeed overnight. The rest doggedly keep at it, get day jobs, or head "back East" to save up more money and try again.

Our life in Los Angeles was rich, but it lacked perspective. Most of the people we knew were under forty. So, when my therapist introduced me to Sister Margaret, my hopes were high for a deep connection with someone who had the perspective of a lot of life behind her.

I drove the thirty miles to my first meeting with Sister Margaret, arrived twenty minutes early, and parked across the street, using those minutes to quiet my rapidly beating heart. I was nervous about meeting this woman; I wanted her to like me. I crossed the street to the Villa, and Sister Margaret greeted me on the concrete walkway beneath towering evergreens. "I am so glad to meet you." She opened her arms wide to usher me inside.

Sister Margaret is small, humble, unassuming, and filled to the brim with quiet delight. When we met, she had been a nun for sixty-five years. We sat opposite each other in comfortable chairs in front of an empty hearth. Through the window I could see the bright green and red leaves of a poinsettia, and through that, the green grass. Sister Margaret asked me to light a candle, and we prayed.

In that season I was impatient with my own lack of transformation. I could see signs of growth: I felt safer in the darkness and I experienced more love and joy than I had in prior months, but I was still struggling. *Can't I just fix this and move on?* I wondered. *What else do I need to do to heal and change more quickly?* I interrogated myself daily.

As my impatience became apparent in our conversation about life and faith, Sister Margaret said something to me that I have found myself saying to other people, and to myself, many times in the years since: "This earth is very old, and our God is very patient. God is a gardener. Gardeners don't go around kicking the cabbages and telling them to grow faster."

When I closed my eyes to pray with her that morning, I saw in my mind a great tree, and I thought of this great, old earth. The tree in my mind was tall like a mountain and dressed in a pattern of green boughs. It was quite still, but I knew, beyond my ability to perceive, it was stretching ever taller with the turning of the earth.

A few weeks later, at a Kairos worship gathering, one of our pastors spoke about being oaks of righteousness. Afterward, as we sang, I again closed my eyes, and a prayer settled on my shoulders like a shawl: *God, grant me the faith of an acorn.*

Small enough to nestle in the palm of my hand, acorns grow into trees large enough to shelter a family from sun or storm. From what we know of them, they do so without planning or effort on their own part. They don't have to will themselves to grow faster. They are subject to the wind and the rain and the soil and the sun and they *will* grow,

Invitation to Practice: Prayer of Acceptance

How do we practice acceptance of what God is—and isn't—doing within us?

See p. 187

quickly or slowly. They submit themselves to burial beneath the soil, to the breaking of their skin and their hearts, and so begin their lives as trees. Years turn to decades, and they grow taller, soaking up only what comes to them—there is no thought of running after what they need for growth, only a slow, upward journey toward the light. As they grow taller, so they grow deeper, roots digging ever more surely into the soil that will offer everything they need to live, or won't, and that will be the end and they will break and fall and rot and become new life and sing new songs as insects and grubs and salamanders.

The next time I visited Sister Margaret, I told her of my acorn prayer. She smiled her sweet smile, and said, "Come." She led me out of the house, down through the garden, and around a corner to a nook under the evergreens. "Look," she said. "I brought this home as an acorn. I didn't think it would grow, but I planted it anyway, and look!" In a large pot was a miniature oak. Only three feet in height, it had the gnarled, scrappy look of the black oaks of Yosemite. It had few leaves, and fewer branches, but it was a living, breathing tree before us. "Someday, it will outgrow its pot," she said, "and then I will plant it in the ground."

I drove home under the bright blue sky. I wondered, *what does it look like to grow like an oak? To let go of responsibility for my own transformation and just to allow myself to be loved?* I didn't know yet, but I would continue to make space in my life for this God I wanted so desperately to know. I prayed, *God, grant me the faith of an acorn, that I might find life in death and trust that I will grow, like a river awash with rain, without striving.*

BREATHE

A PLAY IN ONE ACT

Setting: A shady bench at the top of a park overlooking downtown Los Angeles. A dusty mid-morning.

God: *I love you.*

Me: *...*

God: *I love you.*

Me: *...*

God: *I love you.*

Me: *...*

Me: *I love you.*

God: *...*

Me: *I love you.*

God: *...*

Me: *I love you.*

God: *...*

God: *I love you.*

Me: *I love you.*

God: *I love you.*

Me: *I love you.*

God: *I love you.*

Me: *I love you.*

God: *I love you.*

WHAT WOULD IT LOOK LIKE to make space for God? I was becoming braver in my time alone and more comfortable on my "field trips" with God. I needed more time.

I mentioned this to Dave. "There are some great retreat centers around here," he told me. "Maybe you could visit one."

I did some research, and I booked a private room for two nights at a retreat center on the coast. What would I do alone with God for so long? I didn't know. Perhaps the doing wasn't up to me.

I arrived at night. It was a disorienting drive in the dark, along unfamiliar freeways. I parked and unloaded my car, wandering the complex of buildings with my bags and backpack until I found the lockbox with a key inside. I opened my room—neat, small, grandmotherly—and dropped my bags. Then I walked to the edge of the hill and lost my breath to the city stretched below. There was so much light between here and downtown Los Angeles; I am ever astounded at the sheer size of this city.

My soul mirrored the landscape. Vast stretches of unfamiliar territory, snaked with winding freeways of doubt and fear, lay between my heart and the home I sought. Where was I? What was my good way through? And what was waiting for me at the end? I had come on this retreat to try to sort through some of the mess inside myself. I knew that somewhere along the way something in me had broken, and this was one more attempt to make space for it to mend.

I prayed this prayer before I lost myself in sleep: *"Gentle me, Holy One, into an unclenched moment, a deep breath, a letting go..."* [1]

I awoke with the need to move. Sister Margaret had advised me the week before not to have an agenda for my retreat, but just to invite God into my day. Following her advice, I walked out the door with nothing but a key in my pocket and ran toward the ocean, inviting God along.

Invitation to Practice: How to Craft a Spiritual Retreat

How do we create space for God to meet us?

See p. 189

---

1   Loder, Ted. "Guide Me into an Unclenched Moment." Guerrillas of Grace. San Diego, CA: LuraMedia, 1984. 23. Print.

I ran down, down, down the dirt path. What freedom, what joy it is to feel the strength of my own body! The sound of my breath and the rush of my blood and the waves of the ocean washed me; they released me. Five miles later, I stood on a ledge twenty feet above the crash of the waves. I joined the starfish clinging to the rocks below in their song of praise to the maker of ourselves and this day. I sang aloud, trusting the crash of the ocean to drown out my voice before it reached the ears of any passersby. And what did it matter? I was here, in myself, whole and separate from any other, connected only to earth, star, rock, and wave. Nothing mattered but the song.

I stretched my limbs in the sun and let the wind dry my sweaty body. A family passed on the beach below. "Don't jump," the father smiled up at me, "we still love you!" I laughed with them, warmed by this strange love. The words were easier to accept from the mouth of an unknown father than they were to offer to myself.

The run back up was long and hard in the best of ways: the sun and the sweat and the dust and thirst and the power of my legs to climb. I returned to my room, showered, and ate lunch on a rock while I watched the city below. My food tied me to my home: an apple and tempeh from the farmer's market, brie from the food pantry where I volunteered, and bread baked with hand-ground wheat by old friends. I fought the familiar urge to accomplish something productive. I wanted to analyze, to synthesize, to sort out the messy closet of my overwhelming emotions, organize them, and lock them back inside where they wouldn't be a nuisance. Instead, I walked two miles for a bottle of juice. As I returned to the brink of the hill, I watched the great orange ball of the sun fall into the water behind a thin line of black cloud. I sat on the edge and leaned into the splintering wood of the guardrail. I breathed in the salt wind and watched the ravens ride it, wings outstretched. Eventually, stars peeked out from behind the deep pink clouds. I walked home slowly, lingering at every friendly tree, rock, and hollow. I smelled what mid-November flowers I could find.

I went back to my room and closed the door to the night. I drank two cups of tea in the armchair under the reading lamp and read a novel. Just before bed, I knelt on the edge of the hill and prayed over the city. I slept.

I awoke to rain. I slipped on a rain jacket and returned to the trail of my run. I was utterly alone with the wind and the wet and the green-gray sea far below. I ducked under a tree for shelter, breathing in the damp scent of the thirsty earth. Then I ran.

I ran along the edge of the hill and watched the ocean seize and roll. The wind whipped my wet hair around my face, in and out of my mouth. Suddenly a laugh ripped through me from belly to eyes and I opened arms wide to the wind.

At last I reached my destination—a pepper tree at a bend in the path I had noticed the day before. The rope hung still, a stick tied at the end with a knot above—a simple swing, like the kind that hung along the lake path I grew up near, but never had the courage to swing from. I grasped the knot with both hands. On my second leap, I stayed suspended, spinning with the wind and the mist and the watery light. My soul sang the mist and the water and the light and the air above the light and the One above that and together we sang and danced and spun and were washed in the rain, washed clean, made whole. The tree swayed in the wind, tiny leaves fluttering madly on ancient branches. The rain drummed down on the earth, now masking the ocean in a gray mist. I lingered, suspended in time and space, bare to the One who created both.

It was time to leave. I eased myself down to the earth again, both full and empty. I wrapped my arms around the tree in gratitude. The wind came and whipped the cords of my hair around the trunk of the tree and pushed against my back and held me there, pinned to the tree in a firm embrace. For a moment, I know what it is to love God.

I came away from that place, beaten by the wind and the rain, and found a coffee shop where I could dry off, warm up, and write. I looked out the window, surprised that the ocean, hidden by clouds until minutes ago, was farther off than I had imagined.

It takes time and space to hear the voice of God. It takes patience to experience God's assurance. I had to quiet my own inner voices in order to tune my ears to the frequency at which God speaks to me. For me, that meant engaging my body and freeing my mind. It meant carving out two whole days with no agenda—not an easy task in a busy life. It meant being brave enough to be alone with my own heartache. In solitude, in wind, and in rain, I found at last the presence of God, which had been there all along.

That was years ago now, and I have never been back. Yet, I am always there: held, suspended, embraced by this love that washes and drives and keeps me. I was utterly alone, bare before God and held, loved. You don't get moments like this every day or even every year. How do you hold onto them? How do you live every day out of that deep sense of belonging? To know we are beloved at the core—there is no greater gift.

THE EIGHTH GRADE DANCE

EYES
When I stop to look at your eyes,
I notice.

Your eyes are merry and blue—
they flick around the room as you sing
softly to yourself
and often look up at me.
What is it that you look for
when you look at my face?
A smile?
Merry eyes shining back that you're OK?

And you—
your eyes also
dart to me often,
but with your dark eyes, it's sideways—
furtive, perhaps.
And what is it that you look for?
Approval? A nod?

And you—
you laugh with the best,
eyes dark brown and carefree,
and when you laugh,
you look to my face—
what is it that you hope to see?
Do you hope to share
this laugh together,
pleased with yourself that
you got the joke?

And you—
you laugh, too,
but it's a softer chuckle.
You look up cautiously,
perhaps just to check,
to make sure I'm laughing, too.
What is it that you look for?
Hoping to see
to be seen
to see yourself be seen?

I ask because I know
I know that look in your eyes—
I see it in my own.

Though I may seem distant
we are the same, you and I—
and you, and you, and you, too—
I, too, want to be seen
and so I look at you.

FOR SEVEN YEARS, I had the best job in the world. I cannot imagine loving anything more—except, perhaps, what I'm doing now. There were hard days, and the piles of grading were never fun, but many days I could not believe I actually got paid to teach.

I was born to teach middle school. Most of the time, when I tell people I was a middle school teacher, their reaction is either, "Oh, I'm sorry" and a shake of the head or, "Wow, you must be a special person!" with wide eyes. This is strange to me. Yes, twelve-going-on-thirteen is a very difficult age to be—you couldn't pay me enough to go back to it—but it is a fabulous age to teach.

Seventh graders are the perfect blend of adult and child. Once, a student came into class thrilled that he had won the quiz game during Campus Christian Fellowship at lunch: "Look what I won!" he grinned, holding up a lighthouse keychain. Fifteen minutes later, we were discussing the tragedy of human trafficking and its implications for the lives of middle schoolers in our community. Seventh graders are adult enough that their eyes are opening to the reality of the world around them. They are capable of thinking abstractly and having meaningful conversations, and yet they are young enough that the child in them still shines through.

One of the best parts of teaching was when kids came to me with their problems: friendship woes, home life challenges, and difficult decisions. They needed someone to listen and ask questions. Middle schoolers are generally terrible listeners; they talk over each other, competing for attention. They are effusive and loving, but they are not patient. Many of them are also beginning to pull away from their parents. Having an adult listen, ask questions, and offer simple advice or affirmation stabilizes their shifting worlds.

That school year, the year that would become my last in a classroom, my friendship with Stephanie deepened.

Stephanie and I had worked together since I'd started teaching. We had carpooled my first year. We were always friends, and I liked her, but we hadn't spent much time together before experiencing infertility together. More than anything, I knew she had a sweet soul and she loved God and loved her students, and it was nice to know she was across the building if I ever needed anything.

That was the key to this sudden blossoming of our friendship—I had begun to need in a new way. Like with Abby, I took tentative steps toward Stephanie, and she welcomed me with open arms.

We spent time together, and we talked about infertility. Stephanie was further along in her journey than I, and she was open about her pain. She helped me uncover my own. The naming of the pain didn't lessen it, but made it redeemable; it allowed me to find the dark gifts inside.

Our friendship reminds me of a time in college. I had a hard night, and a friend of mine drove across town to go for a walk with me in silence. I needed to walk in the dark, and her silent presence made me safe. That's what Stephanie and I do for each other.

When I try to think back to how this deepening of friendship happened, it is difficult to remember. Slowly, we moved toward each other. We gave each other hugs in the staff room as we made our cups of tea during the morning break. We went out for coffee. Once, we decided to go out for sushi after school. We arrived at our chosen sushi restaurant only to find it closed, so we went to Trader Joe's next door and bought a package of sushi there, sharing it at a table in the sunny plaza outside. We made the best of things together. We read poetry and discovered spiritual practices of art. We listened together to what God might be saying to us in our shared grief.

One day Stephanie came to my house and confessed her fear of her own darkness, her vast capacity for anger and grief. We cried and held each other—her fear was all too familiar. We kept each other safe in those places, holding each other's stories and each other's pain. We loved one another well. We showed the tenderness toward each other that we had yet to learn to offer ourselves.

Invitation to Practice: Collage Paintings

How might I hear God in a new way?

See p. 194

Of the many things that came out of my years of infertility, Stephanie's friendship became the greatest gift of all.

Each January, Stephanie organizes the Eighth Grade Winter Formal. I chaperoned many times, loving to see the kids all dressed up. They always looked so adult in their dress-up clothes: For many, this was the first formal event they attended without their parents. They were giddy with excitement and full of awkward uncertainty.

That year, the year that would be my last in teaching, I was still trying to become pregnant. January 31 would be our first infertility appointment. January 27 was the eighth grade dance.

Most years, I chaperoned the dance for the obligatory hour and a half and then went home. This year, I wanted to be there for the whole thing—to celebrate with Stephanie what fun we could have with our students.

Stephanie and I got ready together. I borrowed a formal-but-tasteful dress from a friend who has the best collection of fancy dresses I've seen in a real person's closet. I wore Stephanie's bright-red lipstick; she wore hot pink. After I admitted I had no idea how to use a curling iron, Stephanie did my hair. Her bathroom filled with the smell of beauty products, and we emerged from the haze of hairspray and laughter ready to have fun together.

The dance is held every year at the War Memorial building. It is a high-ceilinged room of wooden rafters and glass, perfect for a dance. It was decorated with balloons and lined with tables of food on one end, a DJ on the other.

We checked in the kids at the front table, then circulated among the circulating students. It took two hours of music before any of the students started dancing—mostly they just walked around and looked at each other. *Keep moving*, the middle school mind says. *Keep moving and it won't be awkward.* I remembered my own eighth grade formal, dancing awkwardly with a boy for the first time, but mostly giggling and with my girlfriends. Stephanie and I danced together, roping little huddles of girls into joining us. Eventually they loosened up, and we, the other teachers, and the principal (all dressed for the occasion), took turns breaking up the suddenly very hormonal teens. The windows began to fog around the sea of dancing, sweaty bodies; kids drew pictures and signed their names in the steam. Others hovered by the snack table, downing brownies, strawberries, and sodas.

When the dance closed down at nine o'clock, we waited on the cool darkness of the lawn with the giddy kids as their parents drove up to take them home. I said goodnight to Stephanie as the last of the kids left, squeezing her tightly before I drove away in the dark.

A few weeks later, in the midst of my weeks of waiting for a second round of infertility tests, I found a slim black folder with gold edging in my school mailbox. Inside was a photo: Stephanie and I, formally dressed, grinning ear-to-ear with our bright lipstick.

Stephanie's friendship is an exquisite gift, wrapped in the broken package of infertility. It was a recent friendship, but on the night of the winter formal, we created a past together. We imagined together what it would have been like to be friends in our early years, and so created history. We giggled, danced and were girls together, simultaneously nurturing the kids we commonly loved.

The best of friendships are those pliable enough to hold both sorrow and joy. As I learned to walk in both with Stephanie, I became braver. I discovered that life didn't have to be either sad or joyful. Almost always, in my experience, it is both. My happiest days always contain a little sadness, even if it's only a pang of knowledge that the day will end. Perhaps more importantly, the reverse is also true. Even the hardest of days hold glimmers of joy if I'm brave enough to look for them. I can grieve and still enjoy the taste of chocolate or the sunlight in the trees. It's not a betrayal. That, perhaps, is the key: Finding joy is not a betrayal of my grief. Our hearts are multifaceted enough to experience both joy and sorrow at the same time, and so, certainly, is God.

When I was young, I saw God primarily in the beauty of nature. I felt God's warmth in the sunshine and God's power in the storm. I still do. But now my vision has sharpened. I see God in my tears. I see God in my questions and uncertainties. I see God as I wipe the kitchen counters clean.

THE WAIT

SEARCHING IN THE DARK

When I close my eyes
  I look for you—
    the light in dark places—
and, sometimes, I see black:
    the backs of my eyelids
    inscribed with the gray-green shadow
    of whatever object just left my vision
      until that, too, fades.
What, then, does it mean
    to look for you in dark places?
I look around, and I see light—
    shining off the edge of my teacup,
    sparkling in the hair of a friend,
    lighting single blades in a sea of grass—
and I wonder
    is it in these places that you speak?
Because if it's there—
    the comfort of tea,
    the warmth of a friend,
    the joy in the grass—
then what of you is left
    behind my eyes?
What of you is left when it's just you
    and me
      alone
    in the dark.
And how do I know you are there?
How do I know
    that you see me
      when all I see is
        black?
Can you see in the dark?
And if you are light
    will I still see you
      with my eyes closed?

What if my hands are open and my feet are bare?

THEY MADE US WAIT a year, as they always do. When you are trying to get pregnant, each month feels like an eternity, and we had to wait twelve of them before we could seek medical help. Twelve months of striving and striving not to strive, of thermometers and tests that always came back negative. Of waiting and longing and holding each other close.

I'd been off birth control since April of 2010. Dave said we should call in April of 2011, but I hesitated. We decided to call in July. That was right about the time I started therapy. There were a lot of things moving within me.

"We'll call you in September to set up your first appointment," they said.

September came. School started. I taught. I prayed. I ran. I cried a lot. I wrote. I had coffee with friends. I went to therapy. I graded papers.

I stopped taking my temperature.

Something had to give. I couldn't keep up the science of it all. "Stop trying so hard and you'll get pregnant!" people said. I didn't believe them for a minute. It's not that easy, and anyway, what does it mean to stop trying? But, for my own sanity, I did need to stop trying to control what was happening in my body, and I did need to stop thinking about it first thing every morning. So, I stopped taking my temperature.

I taught and I cooked and I went to church. I went on regular dates with Dave, enjoying our Dual-Income-No-Kids status. On Labor Day, I ran a half marathon for the first time—exhilarating. It was a little scary and a lot of hard work, but my body did something right in a season when nothing it did seemed right. I ran faster than I thought I could run, and I enjoyed it immensely, even the soreness the next few days that meant I was growing stronger.

September came and went without a call. "We should call them," Dave suggested.

"Not yet."

October brought pumpkin spice lattes and pumpkin bread. (Angelenos mark seasons more by flavors than temperatures.) I immersed myself in school. I took field trips and met with Sister Margaret and tried to rest and to listen. I learned about accepting my own neediness, shame, and fear. I spent a lot of time with Stephanie, and talked to my mom more than I had since we first moved to California. I slowed down, stopped running away from God so quickly. I practiced breathing. I went for runs in Griffith Park with Abby and we watched coyotes and hooted at owls.

October ended. "We should call them," Dave suggested.

"Not yet."

I rediscovered parts of myself that had been lying dormant, like my love of poetry and my love of nature. I painted, collaging images on top of each other, listening to what they spoke to me. "Release," they said.

I went on my first spiritual retreat.

Beloved. The word settled down into my soul as I ran and played and wrote and prayed. *Beloved. You are my beloved.*

My mom gave me a Christmas ornament that had hung on our tree since I was little. It was a cuckoo clock, and written in pen on the back was "Waiting on God's timing, Christmas 1982." I was born in 1984. I hung the clock on a little thumbtack over our bed.

Thanksgiving. Abundance, gratitude, celebration. No phone calls.

November ended. "We should call them," Dave suggested.

"Not yet."

I knew Dave was right. We should call, but I didn't want to call. Calling would mean infertility treatment would start, and treatment starting would mean eventually treatment ending, and if it ended without a baby that would mean there was nothing more we could do. I wasn't ready to play our last hand.

In December, my eighty-five-year-old grandfather came to visit. He came to school with me on the last day before winter break and told stories about World War II to my seventh graders. He told stories I'd heard before, and some new ones, and we all listened eagerly. He wore his tweed jacket and his World War II cap, and after lunch he huddled up a little group of boys and he gave them advice, one man to another: Stay in school, work hard, use the gifts you've been given. They were rapt.

I went to see my sister. I read and wrote in coffee shops while she was at work, took naps in her spare bedroom, and played with her husky, Denali, in the snow. I went on a long run along the quiet, snowy highway. I skied in the mountains for the first time. I spent most of the day tumbling and prying myself back up out of the snow, but the sky was crystal blue and the snow was white and soft and smelled like home. We drank hot tea and made an early Christmas feast with Swedish meatballs and a vat of mashed potatoes. We talked of our grandparents, and how happy they would be to see us and the table spread before us.

Christmas itself was muddy. Dave and I went to Yosemite with his mom, and it was a very brown year. Even so, the cliffs and hills were beautiful, and we watched waterfalls and played cards at night over a makeshift picnic dinner in the lodge. One day when Dave and his mom took a short hike, I sat awhile on a cold bench among gnarled, leafless oak trees. Their trunks were black, their brown leaves decomposing on the ground and scuttling across the path in eddies of wind. Oaks are beautiful in their green regalia, but their winter beauty is more haunting—stark, black, naked—their thick, twisted branches exposed, their true shape and stature revealed. They seem older, sadder, wiser. They kept vigil with me in my sadness.

Then it was January. January was time, we agreed. A new year, holiday craziness and travel over, time to move forward. I made the call.

"We are glad you called," they said. "Our system crashed. We lost everything."

"How is the 31st?" they asked. We were free.

We went to our appointment. We answered question after question: "When was the start of your last period?" "Do other people in your family have larger-than-normal heads?" We gave blood and urine for analysis. We listened. Then we waited.

My next series of tests would be one week after my next period. One I dreaded. Too many friends had told me stories of basements with creepy lights and metal tables, of pain and dehumanization. Blood and exposure like childbirth, but without the baby. I was terrified.

A couple of weeks went by. My period was late, but not that late. My sense of calm, my good breathing, my letting go of control crept quietly away. I started to feel ill with worry. I was tired, and more than a little depressed. I stayed home from work one Thursday to sleep off whatever it was I was feeling. I tried so hard not to think I could be pregnant. I wanted to take a pregnancy test, to kill my struggling hope, to prove to myself that I wasn't pregnant and would have to go through the tests and all the rest, that I would not be saved from this. This was my cup to drink.

Thursday night I couldn't take it any longer. Saturday I was supposed to go to a friend's shower, for her second baby, and I was dreading it. I loved her, and I knew it would be a beautiful shower—sweet and prayerful and covered with Pinterest-worthy decorations. I couldn't take it. Friday morning I would take a test.

Dave got up with me very early. We tiptoed into the bathroom together, not wanting to wake our housemates. Dave set a timer, I balanced the stick on the sink, and we huddled on the edge of the bathtub together, holding each other, trying not to hope, only to comfort. The seconds ticked by. Two minutes. I grabbed the stick and saw something I'd never seen before: two tiny blue parallel lines.

"We're pregnant!" I grabbed Dave, filled with joy and relief and anxiety and excitement all brimming over at the same time, whisper-yelling in a cold bathroom very early in the morning, and Dave said, "We *might* be pregnant," and he held me close. And I said, "What do you mean?" And he said, "Sometimes they're inaccurate," and I said, "Inaccuracies are almost always when they're negative," and he said, "Exactly—you said almost," and I said, "We're pregnant!" and he said, "Let's give it a few days before we get too excited." I understood but didn't understand his hesitancy. I was overjoyed—ready to throw off this dark cloud that had been hanging over me for a year and a half and run headlong into excitement, despite fear, despite the probabilities of early miscarriage, despite the .1 percent chance the test was faulty, but Dave wasn't ready for that. That's a difference between us for which we're learning to accommodate: I'd rather feel exhilaration and joy even if it means heartbreak and disappointment, and Dave would rather temper his excitement to lessen the hurt of the fall.

Despite that difference, we held each other, and we were fearfully happy. We went about our days pinching ourselves, reminding ourselves that this, right now, was real.

Saturday's "cute-as-a-button" shower was easy, because I had this quiet, secret joy. I still noticed the centrality of motherhood in all conversations, the knowing glances and nodding heads, but I was no longer so alone. I no longer felt like the strange, empty creature on the periphery.

And yet, I wanted to hold onto the pain of infertility. I didn't want to run headlong into the sunlight, forgetting the road by which I'd come. Too many of those I loved still suffered—from infertility or the desire to be married or other unfulfilled longings. At that shower, I thought of Stephanie, and my heart broke just a little bit. I had wanted her to be first. I had prayed for her to be pregnant first, earnestly. And here I was, enjoying a shower for the first time in two years, everything different for me and everything the same for her. So I held on to a little bit of the pain, kept my heart just a little bit raw and open, kept a space there in that wounded part of me for Stephanie and for all the other people I know who long for children.

The next Tuesday was Valentine's Day. We went to the hospital for an official pregnancy test, which confirmed there was a tiny baby growing in my belly, not quite the size of a pea. I was six weeks pregnant, which meant I had been pregnant at our infertility appointment and didn't know it.

We were overwhelmed with gratitude. For me, it was as if someone had turned the lights on. It almost felt too easy—all that praying and waiting and hoping and suffering and longing and letting go and BOOM! You're pregnant! Quick as peeing on a stick.

Pregnancy affected everything. It affected the way I ate and drank and felt and thought. The leaves swaying in the trees against the sparkling blue sky were more beautiful with the knowledge of this life in my belly. More than anything, I felt rescued. I felt undeserving and grateful.

Even now, years later, I struggle to write about this. Nothing is simple. What does it mean that God, in love and wisdom, chose to rescue me from infertility, but has not rescued so many of the people I care about? I don't ask why, because I am willing to trust the why is beyond my comprehension. But *what*—what does it say about God? I believe God is loving and God is wise and God is a rescuer and a redeemer, making all things new and all things right. That doesn't always mean I get what I want, no matter how good that thing is or hard I pray or how much faith I have (which, for the record, is not always very much). Getting what I want makes me just as confused when I look at the unanswered prayers all around me.

I don't know the answers to these questions, but I do know I met God in a profound way in the months before pregnancy, and my healing started well before Valentine's Day.

I also know this: Getting what I wanted didn't make all of the darkness go away. Just as I had found joy in sorrow, I would find new sorrow even in my joy. Nothing is simple. I had gotten what I wanted, but I was not at my destination; I hadn't arrived. A baby to love would bring great happiness, but it would not answer my questions about self-worth or God's love for me. Motherhood would only make those questions more complex. I would wonder, more than ever, if I was enough for those I loved.

TWO ROADS DIVERGED

FOR STEPHANIE

*You hold my hand in the dark places
and we walk.*

*I was lost
in a catacombs I could not name
and in the naming of it——
together—
we found our way to the surface.
What magic
that in looking at each other
we find ourselves!*

*And we walk
down this open road
after yesterday's
dark tunnel.*

*I walk with you
whether your heart breaks
or mine—we hold
together the broken
pieces, even if
their edges cut
our hands.
I bleed for you.
As he bled, we bleed;
by our wounds and his, together
we are healed.*

*And we walk
under the gnarled oaks of this dark valley,
under the bright sun of that green field.*

*What if your road goes one way
and mine another?
We will still hold hands
as the light fades,
and as a new day dawns.
You, most loyal of friends,
are brave enough to walk with me
where you cannot go
and I am braver for your presence;
I could not walk this road alone.*

*So let us pause
while we still can
and watch the moon together
and breathe in the warm, salt air, rustling
the palms and our hair——
I walk with you;
I wait with you;
together we find our way home.*

TWO WEEKS LATER, I walked into Stephanie's classroom after school. It was brightened by her art as well as her spirit, but this was a heavy day for me.

Today was the day I would tell her I was pregnant.

She was at her desk, grading papers. I took my typical perch on a desk in the front row.

"Hey, friend!"

"Hey! How are you today?"

"I have something I need to tell you… it's still early, but…" I didn't know how to hold my face to show this mix of joy and despair.

"Are you pregnant?"

"Yes."

She jumped up from her desk to embrace me. "Kristen, that is so wonderful. I knew it would happen for you."

She shared my joy; she really did.

It was then my tears broke free—tears of sadness for her, of anger at God that my prayer wasn't answered, of fear for what would become of this friendship. "I prayed, I prayed so hard, Stephanie, I wanted you to be first."

Hers came too, tears of loss. "I know."

I loved Stephanie, so dearly, and I did not want to add to her pain. Soon, my pregnancy would be public, and everywhere I walked I would be followed by a trail of questions: "Boy or girl? Natural or epidural? Have you picked a name yet?" I didn't want to hurt her, and I was terrified to lose her. I was afraid that in this gaining of what I had wanted I would lose what I had found: the gift of her friendship. We had walked through the abyss together, and now I had been set free, but I didn't want to leave her behind in the dark. It was her courage in infertility that gave me mine. We had walked together. Now, I might lose her. I couldn't expect anything else. How could I ask her to walk with me now, when my very body was a living, breathing, growing reminder of her emptiness?

I didn't lose her. Stephanie is one of the bravest human beings I know. As she says, we make each other brave. Ever so carefully, we continued to walk together.

I told her she didn't have to come to my baby shower—I knew what those felt like—and she came anyway.

She was one of the first people to hold our baby after we came home from the hospital. She brought us meals when we were still unable to function. She was the first person outside of our family to put our child to bed away from home.

We continued to talk openly about her infertility. I held onto my wounds, sharing in her sorrow just as she shared in my joy. We pursued each other, relentlessly determined to make this friendship work. We each had a task: to hold space for each other's stories as they diverged. Her task was the harder.

Stephanie is brave.

When I became pregnant, the landscape of my heart shifted from darkness to daylight. I wish I could say it was all the hard work I did, all the prayer and the therapy and the art and the sitting-in-the-pain that allowed me to feel freely joyful again, but it wasn't. If I'm honest, circumstances brought me out of that place. That worried me at first—what if circumstances change, and I end up back in that place? What if I haven't been transformed, only rescued? Is there a difference? It was Stephanie who told me not to worry. The practices that had carried me in my season of darkness would still be there when life took me back to that place. God would still meet me. God is faithful in both our sorrows and our joy, which, most of the time, are all mixed up together anyway.

I would have a child, but that was not my destination. Nor was it, alone, evidence of God's faithfulness. As we continued to walk together, Stephanie and I would find that evidence: As we continued together to open ourselves to God's love, we would be transformed. Though our paths diverged, our transformation would be astonishingly similar.

Being with Stephanie helped me to keep my wounds open—even in this joy, I didn't want to anesthetize the pain or forget the darkness.

Late in my pregnancy, when I was enormous and uncomfortable and oh, so obviously with child, Stephanie asked me to come to her

Invitation to Practice: How to Bless a Friend

What does it look like to bless a friend?

See p. 196

classroom after school one day. "I want to anoint you." She took fragrant oil in her hand, and she blessed me. We were standing on the same patch of carpet where I had told her of my pregnancy months before. I felt her love, her warmth, and the inevitable love of God flow through her and over me. It was a consecration of this friendship, a confirmation that she was not going anywhere. "Peace fill you—flood you—flow through you," reads the bottle of anointing oil she gave me for my thirtieth birthday. That is what her love has done for me. She is strong; she is unshakable; her courage makes me brave. She is loyal in the face of great loss, and we are closer now than we've ever been. Our friendship was forged in the fires of infertility, it survived the rift that was pregnancy for me, and every day it deepens.

Dearest Stephanie, your love has made me more myself. What greater gift could there be?

In that moment of anointing, Stephanie became the hands and voice of God, reassuring me that I was, more than anything, beloved. I felt a darkness lift. Whatever lay ahead would be different. The season of disappointment was over. What was still to come would be difficult—more so than I could have easily imagined then. But it would be different. I was now safe in the knowledge that I was God's beloved. I was equipped with practices that made that knowledge real to me. Never before had I been wounded enough to open my heart so deeply and allow myself to be so loved by God. I would need that love to carry me in the months to come.

II.BORNE IN DISILLUSION

Because you are my help,
I sing in the shadow of your wings.
I cling to you;
your right hand upholds me.
Psalm 63:7-8

SLOW WALKS AT THE MALL

STEEP
Time, it's time.
It's time.
The sun sparkles in your dragonwell,
and my rooibos tastes faintly
of Big Red gum.
Time so rich, so short
like being with myself in thirty years,
or so I hope.
Your advice comforts;
I am glad you are here.
This was the right time for you to come——
there is nothing quite like
a mother's love.
I am glad
you are here
with your eyes sparkling over your cup of dragonwell,
and your hands,
so like my hands,
holding the cup close.
When you leave,
I will look at my hands
and see you in them
and remember
that I will be okay.

I LOVED BEING PREGNANT. I felt terribly sick, but I was also in my element: planning, preparing, making lists, and marking calendars. I had waited long for this role. I read all the right books about pregnancy and parenting. I stayed active. I chaperoned a group of forty eighth graders on a trip to Washington DC and kayaked in the Channel Islands with our church friends. I flew home for one last visit to Wisconsin so our families could see me pregnant. Cousins, in utero, met for the first time. One last flight took Dave and me to the Northwest for ten days of adventuring together—our "babymoon."

The afternoon we flew home from Portland, something shifted. I had pain in my belly. I called the doctor. "Please come in right away so we can make sure everything is OK." We walked the two blocks to the hospital.

The nurse strapped monitors to my belly while Dave held my hand. Tentative relief trickled through us as we heard the tiny heartbeat on the monitor.

"The baby is OK, but you are having contractions. We want to monitor you for a while to make sure they aren't progressing," the doctor told us. It was July 17—our baby wasn't due for another three months.

That day marked the beginning of a season of prayer and helplessness. We prayed for August—by August 15, our baby's chances of survival would increase dramatically. I was not put on bed rest, but was instructed not to exercise: "Watch movies and eat popcorn. Maybe go for slow walks at the mall," our doctor advised.

My desire for pregnancy had been fulfilled, but all was not as it should be. I was not as I should be. I yearned to be a capable, competent mother, but even in pregnancy I didn't live up to my own expectations. The disillusionment began.

I had to get ready: clean the house, buy baby clothes and wash them, prepare birth announcements, organize a space for the baby, find a crib and a bouncer and a breast pump and half a dozen pacifiers. Instead, I sat on the couch watching movies. It was infuriating. Each time I visited the doctor, the nurse asked if I exercised. Each time, I replied, "The doctor told me not to." This landed me on a mailing list for exercise propaganda. Wall posters promoting running mocked me from my mailbox.

I spent my days on the couch, battling the oppressive heat of that summer with two fans and a bucket of ice water. I filled my time with mildly interesting TV shows on Amazon Prime. Another pregnant friend and I watched action movies together—the entire Bourne Trilogy one week—sitting in her air-conditioned living room with bowls of popcorn.

My purpose aside from physically growing a baby dissolved.

Desperate for some new kind of God-connection in my idleness, I painted. I read one poem every day and painted a watercolor in response.

There, I found solace. Stephanie painted with me, and we shared our paintings with each other—radically different in style and form, but similarly poignant.

I brought my book of paintings each time I visited Sister Margaret. She flipped through them, marveling at each, as if she were unearthing a treasure.

Invitation to Practice: Daily Art
How can I connect with God as my identity is shifting?
See p. 200

As I wallowed on the couch, news came that Abby, my dear friend-turned-housemate, was moving. She would be leaving very soon. We celebrated and grieved together, soaking in our last moments as housemates. One day at the end of July, she packed up her Jeep and drove away, leaving me with salt on my cheeks and the lingering scent of anointing oil on my forehead. We had anointed each other in prayer just before she drove away, sitting knee-to-knee under the stained-glass window.

Abby's move opened up a way for Dave and me to stay in our intentional community after the birth of our child. Her back house became ours.

The prospect of a move at nearly eight months pregnant while couch-bound, even a move of forty-two feet, was daunting. Dave slowly filled boxes and stacked them in the living room. I helped as I could, mostly pointing to things from the couch. We asked our friends to come help us on our moving day, trusting in their grace and compassion to get us through.

We had good reason to trust. When we had moved from Pasadena to East Hollywood three years earlier, Dave had woken up at four o'clock the morning of the move with the stomach flu. We put him to bed in Mike and Maria's apartment down the hall and moved without him. I will never forget our friends asking me to come into the bedroom of our new house, screwdrivers in hand: "Tell us where you want the bed. We're going to put it together for you." Thanks to the kindness of many friends, we had a bed to sleep in that night.

This move to the back house was chaotic. I am an over-preparer, and I like to be ready for a move; I don't like sticking final things in boxes when help arrives to pack the truck. This time we were nowhere near ready. We had packed some boxes, but only a few stacks. We hadn't even touched the kitchen. Everything was a mess, and I was stuck on the couch. Suddenly my neediness was not something I could hide within my heart; it was exposed, sprawling all over our living room.

The movement of the next three hours was miraculous to watch. Boxes moved, then dressers and furniture and piles of clothes. Someone followed behind with a broom and a dustpan. Soon, our bedroom was empty. Our kitchen was packed and moved and cleaned. Our crib, a hand-me-down from friends, was assembled upstairs. In the space of three hours, our life had been packed up and moved across the yard and was being put together again. Our Los Angeles family was taking care of us.

My mother and sister arrived two days later. By the time Dave came home from work, they had unpacked, organized, and put away our entire kitchen. We went to Home Depot for cans of spray paint, and much of our old, tired furniture was made new—shelves and dressers we had found on the curb or inherited from friends suddenly looked like matching sets from Pottery Barn (at least from a distance). I watched and advised.

Pregnancy forced me to my knees. I learned to recognize and accept the love of both my family and our community in Los Angeles. I was helpless, I was insufficient, and yet God carried me in their hands.

Self-sufficiency has always been a high value of mine: I want to be competent and capable. I want to have my crap together and to help other people with theirs. When I became pregnant, I thought my struggle with self-worth was behind me. I could move on from my depression. I would get to be a mother, to fulfill a dream I had imagined from childhood. Instead, I found out I would not be able to care for my child—or even myself—as I desired.

In pregnancy, my helplessness was exposed, which allowed me to be tangibly loved. Self-sufficiency is a myth, and a dangerous one: It keeps community from blossoming. Community blossoms out of the soil of need. Even more importantly, I can't accept the love of God without also accepting love—and therefore help—from other people.

Our needs grew, and we were carried by the strong arms of the community around us. God was taking care of us.

TWO BIRTHS

DEATH IS ESSENTIAL
by Stephanie Jenkins

death is essential:
winter barrenness
surprises us
with its graceful dance
of naked limbs
stark against the sullen sky

we need to be drawn
into the stripped-down
structure of things
undistracted
by emerald leaves
and bright bird song

we need to be drawn
to life
below the surface
down
into the core of the earth
spreading our roots deep
tapping into ancient wisdom
buried below layers
of snow and decay
under the shallow scab of frost
into the darkness
 rich, warm, fertile
hidden in the center

death is essential:
it is the unraveling
of our security blanket
a descent
 into the darkness of our birth
a letting go
of things that tangle
a free fall
into the abyss
into the mystery that IS

so let gravity
take you
strip you
let the trappings of your former life
fall away
until naked
you are clothed
in the great unknowing
until falling
you awaken
to flight

THERE WERE VATS of Thai food. Looking around, Dave and I knew we'd be eating pineapple fried rice for weeks. We had invited a group of old friends from our church in Wisconsin to have dinner under the trees in our yard on this hot October night. They were in town for a conference. Happily, the group included my mom. It was a strange and wonderful feeling, this injection of our old life into our new one, a coming together of two worlds, like a wedding or two rivers merging.

I clutched Dave's hand under the table, squeezing hard whenever my belly contracted. The contractions were painful today. I'd been having them now for seventy-eight days—a persistent, uncomfortable squeeze of the belly that kept me on the couch most days, in fear of the safety of this baby. Now they were different.

Two months earlier.

It was another hot August day, so we set up a table under the trees. We filled the table with books, magazines, and tubes of paint. Stephanie was crafting her final project for her Grief, Loss, Death, and Dying class. I was painting national park vistas to hang above a crib.

Stephanie tore pages from books—images of beetles, skeletons, and the Madonna littered the table. We pinned them down with rocks to keep them from fleeing in the hot breeze. She looked at the blank canvas questioningly, but it offered no help. Where to begin?

"Are you ready?" one of our guests, an old friend, asked.

"So ready," I replied, hand on tight belly. "If only because of the heat. I could use a day or two in air conditioning."

"Eat a whole pineapple," he grinned. "It worked for my wife!"

When we'd eaten our fill of curry and laughed with old friends under the garden lights long enough, I said goodbye to my mom. She would get on a plane the next morning, perhaps the hardest thing she'd ever done. She squeezed me hard. "Be safe. We are praying for you." I squeezed back, grateful for her understanding that Dave and I wanted to be alone for this.

We watched our guests depart. Then we walked to the store to buy pineapple.

Stephanie arranged and rearranged pictures on her canvas, opening herself to a vision of grief. I painted with careful brush strokes, creating smooth, flat lines, like a paint-by-number: a dark woods; a green hill; a tiny cabin with lights inside.

I passed her the glue.

I cut up the pineapple and went to bed. I would eat it in the morning.

I chose a second, larger canvas, and began with a smooth blue sky. Stephanie moved from glue to paint, mixing deep reds and purples. She traced the images in black, drawing the scraps of paper, torn from other stories, together into a sea of grief on canvas. What did it mean that I would soon be holding a child, and she would continue to hold this grief? I didn't know. We worked silently together under the trees.

I awoke in sudden pain, like waking with the stomach flu in the night. I curled on my side and breathed deeply: *hee hee, hoooo. Hee hee, hoooo.* I clutched my belly until the pain subsided, and I slept—only to wake seven minutes later, again awash with pain.

After an hour or two, I woke Dave, knowing I could no longer do this alone. He held my belly as I paced the room, then pressed gently on my lower back, adding counter-pressure. He breathed with me: *hee hee, hoooo. Hee hee, hoooo.* I timed and counted and timed. Seven minutes. Ten. Seven. Nine. Thus, the long night passed.

———※———

I layered gray and white, shaping the great mountain. I remembered being there one year before. The trip had been a consolation: not pregnant? Let's camp and kayak in Alaska. I thought of the life within my belly, of the stories we'd tell this child of the places painted on the wall.

Stephanie worked quietly in the dappled sunlight.

———※———

Morning, and no change. I obsessed over the clock, waiting for contractions to come the prescribed three-to-five minutes apart. Five minutes. Seven. Nine. I put away the clock.

At noon, we went to the hospital anyway, four centimeters dilated. My body pulsed and throbbed. I was ready for the pain to go away.

"Go for a walk," they told me. *Walk? Can I still walk?* We walked the circle around the hospital's garden, pausing every half-circle to stand and breathe. *Hee hee, hoooo. Hee hee, hoooo.* I clutched Dave. I clutched a garbage can. *Hee hee, hoooo. Hee hee, hoooo.* Seven minutes. Ten. The contractions refused to come any faster. Finally, on the verge of collapse, I went back inside.

"I'm ready for the epidural," I said.

I waited on the bed and slowly turned to ice. "It's cold," I said. The nurse brought me a warm blanket. "Still cold," I said. She piled more blankets on my legs while my teeth chattered. Bon Iver played quiet songs of winter and I closed my eyes, listening to the rhythm of the steady underwater heartbeat on the monitor.

Finally, they came with the epidural. Warmth flooded my body. I slept.

———※———

I painted the fields below the mountain as I remembered them—an ocean of red and gold, dotted with tiny ponds and patches of green. August, in Alaska, is autumn—a threshold season, blood-red with dying summer leaves. It might be one hundred degrees back home in LA, but Alaska sensed the coming winter despite the still-long hours of daylight.

Midnight came, and it was time to push. The life inside of me was ready to be exiled into the world. Dave and the nurse held my legs and counted: *one, two, three, four, five, six, seven, eight, nine, ten!* "Push down! Harder. Push there! Yes! Those muscles. Hold that! Go! Harder!"

I carefully lettered the name of the park at the bottom: Denali. Slow, thin lines crisscrossed the red-gold field, much more angular and straight than the ambling rivers of Denali I remembered. I looked over at Stephanie. Paint aside, she had again turned to her pile of pictures, searching for the final messages to reveal themselves.

———

Hours went by. At three in the morning, I rested, sitting up to help the baby move downward. He or she was stuck on my pelvic bone. With each push, the tiny body would ease out a bit, enough to see the top of a head, and in each pause, retreat.

They gave me Pitocin, hoping to speed up my contractions, and let me rest. The room was still, except for the typing of the charting nurse. Then suddenly the room flooded with people and light. I felt hands on my body: "Turn her this way, on her side." Dave was elbowed away from the table, fear flooding him, and an oxygen mask was clamped over my face, filling my lungs with cold, rich air. "This way, other side!" Hands were everywhere—turning my legs, my belly, supporting my back, adjusting pillows, threading wires up inside of me. Voices overlapped one another. Someone put a pen in my hand and held out a clipboard. Dave just nodded, wide-eyed. "This is just in case," a voice rose above the others. "It's not an emergency yet."

Eventually, the rapid voices and rush of hands slowed, giving way to quiet. I could hear music again. "Is the baby OK? What happened?" I clung to Dave's hand once more.

"Yes, you're both OK. The heartbeat slowed, so they had to put in another monitor and make sure it sped up again. They think it was the Pitocin. You are both OK."

We waited.

I set my paintings aside and went to the kitchen to pour us fresh glasses of water. The breeze in the trees rippled the shifting patterns of sunlight over Stephanie's hair as she bent over her work. She glued one final piece, then turned the painting toward me, leaning it upright against the tree.

Again, we pushed. And again. And again. My mind grasped at phrases I had memorized, catching few words, but enough. I prayed: *Your strength, not my strength. Your power, not my power. Please, please, please, please! I am not strong enough for this.*

The doctor came in several times to check, and, each time, the nurses convinced her I could push longer. "Watch her push, see? We think she can do this." More hours rolled past. The doctor was caught up in another case, buying us time. I thought vaguely of mountains, of climbing, of running. We listened to four songs on loop—I had brought plenty of Bon Iver and Ryan Adams, but not enough "pushing music." Adele, Florence and the Machine, and Arcade Fire played ad nauseum, but by five o'clock, no one was listening anyway.

At six, the room flooded again: doctors, nurses, techs, residents. Another emergency, or did everyone just want to be there for the finale? The enormous dentist-chair-like light spot-lit my legs.

"This is it," the doctor said. "We'll give you two pushes with the vacuum extractor, then if that doesn't do the trick we'll put you under for an emergency C-Section." Two pediatricians shuffled blankets and instruments around under the warming light in the corner. A resident held the vacuum extractor at ready and waited for the order that never came.

———❈———

"It's kind of morbid," she said.
"It's beautiful," I replied.

———❈———

"Go!" *One. Two.* "Harder, harder!" *Three.* Radiohead ranted in the background. *Four.* "Right there, that's it!" *Five. Six.* "Go! Go! There! Harder!" *Seven.* "Yes! That's it! Come on!" *Eight.* "Harder! HARDER!" *Nine.* "Puuuuuush! Yes!" *Ten.*
"OK, again!"

———❈———

An adoring Madonna was surrounded by a sea of red-purple waves, filled with the crawling creatures who feed on death. She held the Christ-child in her arms. The tiny God's haloed head had been replaced by a delicate white skull.
"I don't know," she said, with a laugh.
"It's beautiful," I said again. "It speaks truth."

———❈———

I feel sliding, a sudden release, and I look up. There, illuminated, is a beautiful little swamp-thing, neck and body wrapped in a purple cord.
"It's a boy," the doctor says.
"His name is Everett." Dave bends his head to me, and I watch tears fall from his laughing eyes.
His name is Everett.

STRIPPED DOWN

FUNDAMENTAL AS WATER

Rain
wakens me in the middle of the night
It has always meant life, growth, refreshment, cleansing;
now it means wet laundry
a trip to the Laundromat we can't afford
because time is precious
and energy dear.

Everything is the same
and yet everything's different.
The same cat is a menace
the same sun is a danger
the same friend, a life-saver.

Never before has a shower felt so good
luxurious water
warm, caressing, cleansing
the scent of soap, satisfying as a meal.

Nothing is the same
and everything is different—

I do not recognize
the face in the mirror.

HIS NAME is Everett.

So began a fundamental shift in myself and my world.

His first few minutes of life were difficult. They whisked my tiny boy across the room to the pediatricians, who hovered over him as he flailed under the bright lights of the warming station. I squeezed Dave's hand and told him to go to Everett. I peered through the crowd of doctors and nurses, trying to get a glimpse of my baby boy, and held the nurse's hand as they stitched me up. I longed to hold my crying baby, but more than that, I wanted him to be safe.

Thirty minutes later, he was snuggling against my chest, the closest he could get to the home from which he'd been expelled. I marveled. Who was this tiny person whom I knew so well and yet not at all?

Our housemates came to visit. The hospital staff brought us a slice of cake with a candle and a bottle of sparkling apple juice. We had a birthday party.

Saturday brought crash-courses in breastfeeding and getting a baby to sleep from a super-human lactation consultant. Then we were launched into the terrifying journey of parenthood on our own, at our own house, without the backup of a hospital staff to fix anything we screwed up. We drove the two blocks to our house, which our housemates had decorated with balloons and streamers and Everett's name on the front door.

We stumbled through the basic acts of caring for a tiny human. The days were a blur. Everett didn't eat well and wanted to be held constantly. We fell into a rhythm that was far from sustainable but allowed us to survive: Dave syringe-fed Everett while I pumped, feeling more like a cow than a mother the first few weeks. Dave was up with Everett until two o'clock most mornings, then I would take over during the day. Sometimes we read poetry together in the middle of the night, the three of us snuggled together on the bed.

Everett napped anywhere the first few months, as long as he was in my arms, which gave us freedom. We walked to coffee shops and went out for breakfast. Our eyes were glazed, our minds foggy, our clothes rumpled and spotted with spit up and milk, but we were out of the house, and that felt good.

I remember distinctly how rested I felt after my first three consecutive hours of sleep. How glorious it was to complete one REM cycle! Dave and I were like tired bumper cars knocking into each other between shifts. *Why didn't anyone tell us* it *would be like this?* we wondered, droopy-eyed. *Would anyone ever have kids if they really knew what it was like?* It was worth it, but it was hard.

Between the hormones and the sleep deprivation, I was an emotional wreck. Everett's inability to nurse made me feel like a failure. I couldn't meet even his most basic needs. "You are all the mother Everett needs," my friend Jessica told me. I tried to believe I was enough mother for him. It wasn't easy.

I was surprised. I knew mothering a tiny baby would be difficult, but I did not expect to feel so incompetent. I did not expect to lose who I was. Again, I found a counterbalance of sorrow with joy. I adored Everett, but this wasn't what I expected. Disillusion grew within me. New motherhood is full of grief—grief at the loss of self, the loss of the life I once had, the loss of our marriage as we had known it, and the confusion of learning to love a little person who is so hard to know.

What surprised me most was how alien my own body felt. It had just done an incredible thing—grown a baby, pushed him out, and nourished him completely—and it was out of control. I was a sticky, milky mess. Showers felt wonderful, but I was usually covered in milk before I'd managed to dry off. On more than one occasion I discovered milk dripping down my belly onto restaurant floors, in parking lots. It was inconvenient. Everett was great in public; I couldn't take me anywhere.

Also strange was the tether that tied me to him so tightly. I thought about him all the time. When friends held him a few feet away, I watched constantly, analyzing their technique. I even did that to Dave, though he was a more capable parent than I was in those first weeks. He read Everett's needs better than I did, and he was more patient in meeting them.

I don't like doing things I'm not good at. I like to be competent. I don't like to start at the beginning or practice or learn from my mistakes; I just like to do everything right the first time.

This made new motherhood difficult, because I didn't know how to do anything. I couldn't even figure out how to eat. My mom came to visit when Everett was three weeks old, and I had a revelation: I can put him down in a baby chair for five minutes and he'll be OK! You mean I don't need to hold him every second and wait for someone to tap in so I can go to the bathroom?

There were many lessons like that, lessons that broke down the myth of my all-importance to Everett. He would be OK without me for five minutes. Eventually, he would be OK without me for five hours!

I thought back too often to his first thirty minutes of life: He was crying, he was afraid, and I was not there. Yes, I was having my insides stitched back together, but he needed me, and I wasn't there. I spent everything I had trying to make up for that.

I have never been more grateful for living in community than I was during that mad, messy time. Our housemates were the family we didn't have locally. One watched Everett until midnight on our first date night, which was rather ambitious: a Mountain Goats concert at the Troubadour. Another took Everett for walks so I could nap. Once, one of them came over to turn off a stove burner for me—I had been steaming beets, but Everett fell asleep in my arms and I didn't want to wake him.

Six weeks. That's what they told me: Survive the first six weeks, and you've made it. It's an insane test to make sure you're qualified to care for a human being. We did survive the first six, and then another six, and then eventually Everett was sleeping through the night (sometimes) and napping like a champ (on a good day).

The first months of parenthood are hard to describe. They are magical and impossible. I constantly cleaned things—diapers, dishes, laundry—but everything was always dirty. I felt invisible. Everett was too young to say thank you or even smile, and no one else had any idea what I did all day. Most days, there was no more to show for my efforts than a crying baby and a cranky Mama. My dad says mothering is an act of holding entropy at bay; it is a cosmic endeavor. But I felt small. I told Dave I needed him to ask me what I'd done when he got home from work every day. I needed someone to know how I'd spent my time. This was a huge shift from teaching, and I needed the validation.

Every summer, the end of the school year feels like a rocket launching into space: loud, fiery, complicated systems all working together to accomplish one final push and then, suddenly, the weightless void. I had decided to leave my teaching job to stay home with Everett, and the void was much larger and more permanent. Suddenly I didn't have 180 thirteen year olds telling me all day that I was OK, that I was smart and funny and competent. I might never have that again. I would have to learn to be OK without it. My identity, so wrapped up in who I was for these kids—nurturer, teacher, mentor, friend—would have to land elsewhere. Mothering didn't feel like enough.

But there was God. In the night, when Everett wouldn't sleep, we whispered to him stories of God's love. I stole quiet moments in God's presence during Everett's naps. We felt the tangible effects of God's love in the hands of friends bringing food, loving arms, listening ears. I understood Jesus and God's love for us in a profound new way. I couldn't think too hard about God's love made tangible in the sacrifice of Jesus, beloved Son, because it hurt too much when I looked at my own son.

Invitation to Practice: **Fight for Rest**

How do we rest in seasons when it feels impossible?

See p. 202

See p. 202

When Everett was four months old, our story took a turn. We had known since his birth that he might need minor corrective surgery, and when he was three and a half months old, the doctor confirmed it.

The story of his surgery is Everett's. Its details are not mine to tell. But, I will tell you a piece of it, because it shaped who I am as a mother. His surgery revealed to me the depth of my desire to be enough for my child, to protect him. I felt a great weight of responsibility and, in time, of guilt and failure.

I am not the mother I long to be. I am not strong enough to protect my children.

Surgery was scheduled for March 13.

I have never been so terrified.

WHAT IF HE DOESN'T WAKE UP?

FOR DAVE
You are my rock.
I know I'm not supposed to say that.

You see my needs
when I struggle to see any needs but his.
You see my beauty
when all I see are means to meet his needs.

You are joy
and strength
and solitude——
or mine, anyway.
I could not do this without you.

You remind me how to see
when I'm buried deep in my day,
eyes closed.
I have measured out my life with baby spoons,
but you pull me up from the ocean floor.

WHAT IF HE DOESN'T wake up? That was all I could think about. Our tiny, four-month-old baby boy—happy, beautiful, healthy—would go under anesthesia and be cut open. I couldn't rescue him, which is what I wanted more than anything to do.

Dave, at the time, preferred to call it an "outpatient procedure," but to me that didn't carry the weight I needed it to carry. It was a simple surgery, one of the ten most common for children under eighteen. We have friends who have gone through much harder medical procedures with their children. For me, it felt momentous. The hardest thing I've ever experienced is watching my child suffer. A friend of ours said once, after his son was in the hospital because of an allergic reaction, that he thinks most wars are started over seeing our children in pain. I believe that.

The surgery was scheduled only a week in advance. I was grateful for that. I was tortured enough those seven days. I feared, deep in my heart, that this perfect little son of ours was going to die. That he would go under anesthesia and never wake up. That, in signing the papers agreeing to this surgery, it would be my fault.

The Sunday before the surgery, as we sang and prayed, I closed my eyes. An image came to me—a vision, perhaps. Earlier that day, I had practiced contemplative listening in a workshop. We had sat in silence for ten minutes, asked God to be present and allowed the images or thoughts that came to speak to us. Perhaps I was still more open than usual to what God might be saying to me. I had never thought about God speaking through images before.

In this vision, I was holding Everett, swaddled tightly in my arms. I lifted him up, held him out before me, high, offering my little boy up to God. God took my son from me for a moment, lifting him out of my loving arms. Then, God gently gave him back to me. I felt four words settle on my heart: *[Trust this. Trust me.]*

I was still terrified, but that vision carried me through the next four days as we waited for surgery. I hadn't heard God speak in this way before. Perhaps it was a result of my practices of making room for God's spirit, or perhaps God simply knew how much I needed that image and those words. I trusted them with what strength I had.

On Wednesday morning we woke Everett in the dark. Our check-in was at 5:30. We walked up Sunset Blvd. to the hospital. We spent two hours waiting in different rooms—hours of fear and nervous anticipation. We didn't know what to expect. We didn't know when we would say goodbye, or where or how. We didn't know how to hide our fear from Everett. We had packed his favorite books, and we read them over and over. We changed him into "tired tiger" scrubs, far too big for his tiny body. The nurse said he could keep his own socks on—navy blue ones with orange and gray and gold stripes. He played on the examination table, crying little in spite of his hunger and thirst. Dave and I held him, held hands, held our fear at bay as best we could.

Then it was time for us to say goodbye. Dave held Everett close, kissed him, and passed him to me. I clung to him, smelled his honey head, told him how much I loved him. Then I pried him from my arms and laid him on the hospital bed. The resident put up the railing and they rolled him away, through the doors to the operating room. We did our best to smile as Everett began to cry. As soon as the doors swung closed behind him, Dave and I wept. Then we forced ourselves to turn and walk away, to take the elevator down to the waiting room, to trust that, somehow, God was bigger than us and was in this with Everett.

We sat down to wait.

We sat in two chairs, side-by-side, and watched the monitor that showed the patients' numbers and where they were. Everett's number, with a green "OR" next to it. We watched it for two hours. I couldn't read, couldn't write. I could only pray desperate prayers: *Be there, God, take care of him, please.*

I went into a back room to pump. I was uncomfortable, having been unable to nurse Everett for many hours now. I didn't know what to do with the milk afterward.

The surgery took longer than we expected. We talked to the waiting room attendant, and she called the OR. "The doctor will see you shortly," was all she said.

Finally, we got the call that it was over—the doctor would see us now. We went up the elevator, and I fought down the fear rising in my throat. We were seated in yet another waiting room, and then the surgeon came in and sat down across from us.

"The surgery went well," he said. I cried in relief. Why hadn't anyone told us earlier that he had made it through?

We made a few notes on after-care and asked a few questions, and then we waited to be called to see him. They assured us we'd be with him when he woke up.

They were mistaken. At last we were called, and we walked into a chaotic recovery room, searching the curtained-off beds for our little boy. Monitors beeped. Lights flashed. Equipment rolled by on carts. Children were crying. Suddenly it hit me: The hoarse screams coming from the section in front of us were Everett's. A desperate-looking nurse held him tight, bouncing him up and down. She asked, "Are you mom?" I nodded. "Here," she said, helping me hold Everett around the tangle of IV tubes and monitors.

"Can I nurse him?"

"Yes, right away."

Dave and I sat down on two chairs, just inches between us and the hospital bed, our backs up against the curtain behind us. Dave helped me adjust my hold on Everett, and at last our little boy calmed as he filled his hungry belly. Peace overcame his fear and disorientation with this familiar action and familiar place in my arms. We snuggled close, trying to create a bubble of warmth in the awful chaos.

We were discharged quickly, with a box of medication and instructions to come back in a week. We took Everett home, forced several medicines into him, and prayed he would sleep. He did.

That night, our Kairos friends were having dinner across the yard, and Dave and I went over to get plates of food while Everett slept. I sat on the porch for a moment with my friend Michelle. Michelle is a truth-teller. "How are you doing?" she asked. I recounted the events of the day, focusing on Everett and how brave he was. "But how are *you* doing?" she asked again. I couldn't answer.

Everett's surgery changed me. It was a rite of passage, a baptism into a club I never wanted to be part of. Michelle said that night that this one event would affect who I was and how I was as a mother for the rest of my life, in ways I couldn't yet imagine. Years later, the truth of her words is still unfolding.

Over the next few days, the days before my twenty-ninth birthday, I fell into depression. I wanted to eat a lot; I wanted to sleep a lot. We were exhausted. We hadn't realized how difficult it would be to care for Everett in his recovery. His first good sleep had been a gift, but as the medication from the hospital wore off, he was in pain. Dave went back to work too quickly, and we didn't ask for help from our friends. We suffered through nights of little sleep, waking every few hours to wake Everett and force-feed him more medicine. We ate dinner in bed and watched old episodes of *Parenthood*. We numbed ourselves and kept moving. This was not a part of motherhood I had expected.

The undercurrent of my depression was overwhelming guilt. Though I knew it was illogical, I felt it was my responsibility to protect Everett from pain, and I had failed. He had woken from surgery, scared and in pain and disoriented and alone. In his hour of greatest need, I was not there. I was not strong enough to protect him. It brought to mind Everett's birth, when he was crying, checked over by doctors for thirty minutes before I could touch him. He needed me, and I was not there.

Everett's surgery uncovered the lie already lurking inside me. I thought it was my job to shape his life. If I tried hard enough, I could give him a perfect one. If his life was not perfect, I had failed. More than that: I, myself, was a failure.

Dave didn't understand those feelings, but he didn't discount them. He listened with love and gently encouraged me in practices that might bring healing.

Invitation to Practice: Shhhhhh...

How do we listen for the voice of God?

See p. 204

Three days after Everett's surgery, on my birthday, I walked up to Barnsdall Park for a moment of quiet. I brought my journal, filling its final pages with my sadness and fear. I closed my eyes to listen.

I saw Everett, about five years old, running and playing in an empty field. He was alone, or thought he was, and he was happy. Then, circling high above his golden head, I saw bird wings—a red-tailed hawk soared above him, watching with its sharp eyes, protecting him. The image faded, replaced by one of Everett curled in my lap on the couch in front of a warm fire in a stone hearth. *[You will be there.]* I heard. *[I love you, and I love him.]*

I clung to that assurance through the next dark months, believing with all my strength that it was real. I would be there when Everett needed me, but, more importantly, even when he was running alone through a golden field, God would be there, watching. And God was also watching over me.

GUILT IN THE AFTERMATH

GUILT

Guilt's thin, yellow dress hangs from her boney
shoulders,
the sharp angles of her body
pronounced on her frail frame.
She cowers in her battered box
comforted by the soft swish of her hair
against the cardboard.
Her fingers are stained
with the blood of the rotten fruit
tossed by passersby—
they dare not let her die.
Her father, Shame,
stops by to shake a finger,
but her mother, Recklessness,
is nowhere to be found.
Guilt spends her days hiding,
willing herself smaller,
that perhaps she might altogether disappear.
On clear nights she creeps
out of her box in the cover of blackness,
the bottomless black wells of her eyes
wide toward her sliver of sky,
hoping to glimpse the faint shimmering
of a lonely star.

EVEN WITH THE VISION of the hawk to which I clung, guilt consumed me. Looking back, it's hard to explain why. Everett had a minor corrective surgery, which he came through well. Yet, somehow, I couldn't let go of the idea that I had allowed something terrible to happen to him. He was mine to protect, and I hadn't been there when he woke in pain, confusion, and fear. He was no longer in my belly, but I had not released him to the world and the protection of the One who made him.

"The narrative you're telling yourself about Everett's surgery and yourself as a parent is not God's narrative," Dave said to me gently, a couple of weeks later, as he saw me sink into guilt and shame. I started asking God a question: *What story are you writing in this?*

I was exhausted. Everett was needy, uncomfortable, not napping well, and required almost-constant attention. I couldn't shake the messy, dark feelings inside of myself. *I did this to my son,* I thought. *This is my fault.* The truth I had learned about God's love for me in my infertility seemed dim, uncertain. I might be beloved, but would that love extend to my child? Would God carry us when I was too weak?

I dreamed terrifying dreams, my dream-self screaming me awake before the worst could happen, before Everett fell off a cliff or was sentenced to death in some awful court of law. *Save him,* these dreams said. *It's my responsibility to protect my son.*

God spoke to me in visions. This new language was a gift I didn't quite realize I had received. I made space to listen. I closed my eyes and waited quietly for the images to reveal themselves. This felt strange and new, mystical and wonderful, and I wasn't certain how to talk about it. God chose to speak to me in a language I loved—that of metaphor. Metaphor is how I express myself, through art and poetry. It became the way I talked to God.

One day in prayer I saw a heart: a bloody, wounded heart, lying exposed in a drift of snow. As I watched, the blood flowed back inside the heart; the snow first mended it, then melted into the green floor of a quiet forest. *[Remain in me, and I will heal your heart,]* God said. *[I will make you whole.]* God met me in my pain. Even in my disillusion, God promised to sustain me.

Over the course of the next few weeks we realized something was not quite right. Everett's surgery was not healing as it should. We suspected that the surgery had not worked, and he would need it again. On April 10, less than a month after the first surgery, we knew for certain. I was overwhelmed with guilt.

Why guilt? Why not anger? Though I knew on an intellectual level that this could not be my fault, I still, at my core, believed by some twisted reality that it was. Even now, I cannot explain exactly why. Some deep-seated shame about who I was had not yet been overturned. Everett was my responsibility, and I had failed him. Michelle said to me, in the midst of those months of wrestling, "You are a very competent person. God has to take you way beyond the end of yourself to show you how to let go of control. You can go a long way before you reach the end of the diving board, before you even know there is a diving board."

Then came Easter, and Good Friday. Dave went to the Good Friday gathering at Kairos, and I stayed home and rocked Everett to sleep. I pictured Jesus on the cross, more clearly than ever before. *My God, my God, why have you forsaken me?*[1] I mourned over the broken body of my Savior and the not-quite mended body of my child. I pictured God in that moment, as a parent, and I mourned with God and for God.

Then I was angry with God. *How could you, God, who know the pain it is to leave your child abandoned in the midst of the breaking of his body and his heart, ask me to do the same?*

Why? I asked. *Why do this to us?* The closest I heard to an answer was *[Because a world built on sacrifice and love is the most beautiful.]*

Sister Margaret listened to my grief. She said that without suffering there is no resurrection. She reminded me of labor, of the joy and blessing that came out of pain and blood and exhaustion. She said that all Everett needs from me is my love.

She suggested that I draw my feelings. I drew Everett, curled in the fetal position, and myself, curled around him, protecting him with the curve of my body in the middle of a storm. I asked myself, *when did I begin to believe the world was such an evil place?*

Invitation to Practice: Draw Your Feelings

How do we process feelings we don't understand?

See p. 206

One afternoon during Everett's nap I sat down with my journal. At Michelle's suggestion, I wrote a list: What do I want for Everett? I want for him to be healthy and whole. To be good. To be innocent. To be resilient

---

and to trust God to take care of him. To feel safe, loved, and nurtured. To learn how to function well in the world. To feel confident. To know God and walk with God. To be compassionate.

Much of what I want for Everett grows out of hardship. He will not learn resilience if he never struggles. He will not learn trust if he's never afraid. He will not learn compassion if he never knows pain. It is not my job to protect my child, but to teach him how to come through hardship well.

Now I know this: the same is true of me and God.

I will not always be rescued from hard things, but God, with my consent, will always use them for my transformation. We can choose whether to be softened or hardened by our pain. We can choose to find the good way through. It is a difficult road, but there are treasures there when we train our eyes to see. In hardship we learn empathy, tenderness, and strength. When we relentlessly open ourselves to God's love, even when that love burns like fire, we are made new. We become more loving, more honest, more faithful. We become more like Jesus.

I want to find this Way, and I want Everett to find it one day, too.

Another vision came. It came daily for many weeks. I was clinging to the face of a steep cliff, holding onto the rock with just the tips of my fingers and the tips of my toes. I let go—or perhaps I fell, it was hard to tell which. I fell backward, almost floating, a long, long fall. Then I splashed, sinking down deep into warm, salty water. It gurgled around me; then I popped to the surface and felt the warm sun on my face. I felt exhilaration, no fear.

What does it look like to fall?

Every day, I would again find myself on the cliff's face, and again, in my mind I would let go, free-fall, and land with a splash in the warm water. I slowly unpacked new layers of meaning. This vision was about letting go of control over Everett's life. It was about not trying so hard to climb— to change and to grow—but allowing myself be carried by the grace of God. It was about letting go of guilt and shame and splashing into the unfathomable heart of God.

BREAD AND WINE

ENOUGH

I tell you
do not worry about
your life, what
you will do, where
you will live.
Even the most
delicate monarch, who flies
hundreds of miles, has
a place to return
home, in the arms of friends.
Are you not more
loved even than they?

EVERETT RECOVERED from surgery. We knew he would need another, but we wouldn't schedule it for another six months. Life returned, more or less, to normal. Everett and I went on walks again, played in our yard under the trees. We made pictures with finger paint. He learned how to sit up, how to roll.

I read Shauna Niequist's book *Bread & Wine*.[1] *Bread & Wine* paints the table as a place of emotional safety—a place for healing and restoration. One day, as I was reading a simple scene in which the women in her cooking club came to the table together, I started to cry.

Why am I crying?

My tears at the simple description of life around the table awakened me to action. I texted my friend Julia, and together we began a cooking and book club about *Bread & Wine*. We each asked a few friends and let

---

1 Niequist, Shauna. *Bread & Wine: A Love Letter to Life around the Table, with Recipes.* Grand Rapids: Zondervan, 2013. Print.

them ask a friend or two and ended up with a group of six women, most of whom didn't know each other. Stephanie was one of them.

The six of us met together only five times before Jennifer moved to Seattle and the group disintegrated, and yet, it was the safest, most intimate group of women I had ever known.

We met first at Julia's to introduce ourselves and set a reading plan. Julia made delicious, intricate dumplings and I made a cherry cobbler and a salad, splurging on goat cheese and dates from an Armenian market up the street and decorating it with red and orange nasturtiums from our yard.

Our next meeting was at Stephanie's house. She chose to host that evening because it was the night of her brother's birthday—her brother Nathan, who had been killed in a car accident when he was eighteen.

Stephanie has a gift for creating spaces of beauty and openness. Her home is my retreat center; walking in fills me with warmth and love and peace. That night, I entered to the scent of sizzling garlic and ginger and a slideshow of Nathan as a child set up on Stephanie's laptop. Linda arrived with a colorful confetti of salad, complete with a stowaway praying mantis from her walk over. We spent a few minutes trying to evict the little intruder. I stuck two pans of cookie dough in the oven, filling the house with the scent of melting chocolate. Each of us arrived more dressed up than usual, dressing for ourselves and for each other.

Stephanie's backyard is impossibly lovely. It belongs on the cover of a magazine: a terraced landscape of succulents and trees, flowers and lights. She set the stage beautifully that night. Nathan loved Chinese food, so that was our theme, and she had borrowed placemats, chopsticks, and sparklers from Linda's travels in China.

We dined outdoors, under the towering live oak, encircled by its branches. The crisp, fruity white wine Jen had brought was the perfect complement to the hot day. As our plates filled and emptied and filled again, we shared stories about food and our childhoods. I remembered Swedish Christmases at my grandparents' farm, the excitement as a kid of throwing a piece of bread into the pot of duppa and having Papa lift it out for me, gently setting it on my plate, and how much better potato sausage tasted when we pressed it into the casings by hand. I remembered how my dad made us pancakes shaped like animals; on my first Christmas trip back home after moving to California, he made me a reindeer.

The sun slowly set behind the hills and the lights hanging from the great tree took their places. I pulled the pans of cookie dough from the oven and heaped them with ice cream, letting the cold sweetness soak into every crevice of the hot cookie and melted chocolate. I brought them to the table. We dove straight in with our forks, sharing one platter while we shared our unmet hopes and dreams. We talked of love lost and longed for, of children, of death. Each woman brought the raw, uncensored gift of herself to the table—baring hurt, grief, and anger at God. I thought of Everett, and his surgery, and the knowledge I carried that he would need a second. My precious little boy would be operated on once more. We joined hands in prayer, and I felt hot tears roll down my cheeks—tears for the losses of these dear women, and for my own.

Stephanie shut off the lights above, and we stood in a circle in the dark. She read a verse from Isaiah: "The people walking in darkness have seen a great light; on those living in the land of deep darkness a light has dawned."[2] Then she struck a match, and we lit sparklers. They showered our uplifted faces with their audible explosions of light; we laughed, we whooped, and we danced. We drowned out the serenade of the crickets and the hiss of the sparklers with our cries of joy and triumph. We have won! We suffer, we grieve, we cry, and yet here we are in this moment. We have life, we have love, we have food and safety and lights in dark places. Most of all, we have hands to hold and people to cry and laugh with. Even the memory of it now makes my flesh tingle.

Invitation to Practice: How to Make a Friend 2.0 How do we deepen friendships? *See p. 207*

That evening nourished my body and nurtured my soul. I wanted to soak it in, to hold on to it when my days turned bleak. Today I am different because of these women. Today I feel surrounded and held and loved by incredible women—gracious, loving, faithful, kind, beautiful women—women I trust to care for me. I know now that I am worth befriending. Through these women, God has carried me.

That night under the lights opened me anew to the rich intimacy that can be found in friendship—an intimacy that comes, first, from saying "I love you," and, before that, even, from admitting you need it. That is the hardest part. If I were the woman I was trying to be—the competent, capable, perfectly-put-together-woman—I would not have needed these friendships. If I hadn't realized that I wasn't that woman, that instead I was needy, broken, and insufficient, I would have missed this gift. I might not be the perfect mother, but I was loved.

These women were the arms of God on the days when I wrestled with guilt and shame. Through them, I was borne.

I wrote of that night in my journal, and I ended the entry: "I am in awe." As I look back on that brief summer of companionship with those women and the life to which they opened me, I am in awe still.

THERE WILL BE TIME FOR REVELATION

THE INSTANT BETWEEN

I.

I cling to the rock
gripping with all my strength
the tiny holds——cracks and ledges just
wide enough for a finger tip
Aware
only of the rock
and the air
behind, above, below.
Time passes——moments,
or eons, perhaps——
and then there is nothing but air rushing
by my falling body.
Silence.
Heavily weightless, nothing moves but the threads
of my hair, winding and unwinding around
one another in the wind,
a graceful dance.
Splash!
I plunge down deep, feet first
into the warm green water,
silence broken by the cavalcade of bubbles
babbling about me.
Suspended in the instant between
moving down and moving up
I taste the salt, feel it
kiss my lips, sting my eyes.
Then, in a rush, I surge to the surface
and suddenly it is sun, not water, that kisses my face.
I smile
and float,
held by the water, warmed by the sun
on the surface of a vast ocean.

II.

I wake in darkness.
I smell the rich, damp smell of earth
so close to my nose I can hardly breathe.
I can't move enough to open my eyes.
I hear footsteps
muffled just enough
that I cannot tell if they are distant
or just above my head.
A moment passes—
or eons, maybe—
and I can feel a new warmth
stroking my hair.
I am suddenly aware of my arms
and the power to move them.
I push upward
feeling the damp, rich soil
move through my fingertips.
One by one, my ten fingers reach the surface—
there is no hurry here.
And then I discover my legs—
a slow flexing, a memory of movement—
I have done this before.
My legs push down
toes digging deeper into the soil
surrendering to its rich, fragrant darkness.
Time passes
in the in between
and then gradually
or suddenly—
which, I truly cannot say—
I feel the sunlight on my face:
a second awakening.
I blink the soil from my eyes
too accustomed to darkness
to take in all that light.

III.

I cling to the rock.
Or the ladder, rather,
there so long the rock has grown around it.
The waves batter my back
again
and again.
For many moments I can't breathe

I cough the salt from my lungs,
blink it from my eyes—
the ocean has eclipsed all possibility of tears.
I brace myself for another wave—
just time enough to remember how to breathe
and adjust my grip on the cold, ridged metal
between each onslaught.
How long am I here? I cannot say.
Time passes.
Then someone is behind me.
He is familiar, yet I'm not certain I
have seen him before.
He wraps his strength around me,
clinging to the ladder for me
pressing my body to safety
holding it with his own.
"I will hold you to this rock," he whispers,
and in that moment I know his voice.
Time passes. Moments. Eons.
Gently, he pulls me from the ladder on the rock.
We float backward
He holds me in the swell
as my hands remember how to relax their grip.
"It's OK," he says, and I look around.
As he fades into the ocean,
the thought comes to me:
I have been here before.

BY THE GRACE of God, I was carried through months of sadness over Everett's surgery and the impending second one. As much as I was able, I made space for my grief. Every day, while Everett napped, I sat on our front porch. I wrote. I made lists of my fears. I wrote down all the worst things about Everett's surgery—removing the bandage, the exhaustion of recovery, and my fear that I missed out on an important stage of his development because it was overshadowed by this one event. I wrote of my disillusionment, my confusion about who I was and what it meant to be a mother. I made space for God.

I read poetry, my Bible and books about spirituality. I wrote poems when I didn't know what else to write, or lists, or scraps of phrases that came to mind. When I couldn't write, I drew, or sat and listened. Mixed in with grief was the relentless shame I felt. I used metaphors to write about my deepest fears: *I am Edward Scissorhands, unable to touch those I love without wounding them.* I was terrified that my own grief over Everett's surgery would somehow affect him. Dave helped me see that my feelings were stronger than the situation merited. He had grieved deeply, too, but he was OK. He asked me often how I was doing, and continually reminded me that my story of guilt and shame over Everett's surgery was not God's story. I had some deep soul work to do. It would take time.

There's no simple trick to introspection or insight, just a lot of persistence and patience. I asked questions. *Dare I be angry with God? Why does God answer some prayers, but not others? What if I haven't prayed right, or prayed enough, and this is somehow my fault?*

I prayed for God to heal Everett without another surgery. I prayed that he would be spared, that we would all be spared.

Often, when I closed my eyes, I saw a stone wall in an empty field. Everett and I sat on the wall, waiting. He played. I didn't know what we were waiting for.

I was angry, but afraid to be angry. I was afraid that anger with God would distance me from God's love. I worked on owning my anger by writing about it and praying about it and admitting it aloud to people I trusted. I tried to let enough anger out that the shame and guilt underneath were exposed, so I could experience and process them, too. The longer they lingered in the dark, the scarier and more powerful they became.

I read books. I talked with friends. I listened. I remembered the practices God had used to heal me during infertility, and I tried them again. I felt battered by waves of emotion. *[I will hold you to this rock.]* God said. *[I won't let you drown.]*

I read more books. I had late-night and early-morning talks on the phone with my dad. I prayed and listened and waited. I told my story to those who had the patience to sit with me in my grief. I wrote—copying the words of others into my journal when I didn't have my own. I asked God to reveal what needed to be revealed. I listened.

Invitation to Practice: Whispers

How do we tune our ears to the voice of God?

See p. 209

Then one day God wrote me a letter.

Actually, Stephanie wrote me a letter, but never in my life have I heard so clearly from God. It was written in the lovely, personal language of words and images that I had discovered was my secret language with God. I read her letter, God's letter, and I wept in gratitude. Who am I that God would speak to me so clearly through the words of this friend?

This is what it said:

Dear Kristen,

I decided to follow your lead and write a letter by hand to someone I love—you! So thank you; you are always inspiring me towards beautiful activities. You have been my muse, leading by example, to find the space to play with art and words and old books and bits of paper, to use these things as a way to listen more closely, more intently, to the voice of God.

"The soul is hungry for beauty... we feel most Alive in the Presence of Beauty... our frailty is illuminated by a different Kind of Light in which we come to glimpse behind the shudder of appearances the sure form of all things. In the experience of beauty we awaken and surrender in the same act."[1]

I am enjoying the profound ideas of this book, Beauty. I like the idea of awakening and surrendering at the same time; it connects to the lesson I've been learning over the last two years of letting go and receiving. It is this open space of paradox where both light and dark are held at the same time. We need the darkness of soil to grow roots, deep roots to hold us, support us, nurture us. We need also the brightness of sun that coaxes the flower of our souls to bloom. We are growing down and growing up at the same time. There is something about darkness that calls us to the depths of our soul and our selfhood. I know that my own darkness of infertility forced me to go down, down, down to where I felt I lost the light completely, but that process of falling into the darkness, surrendering to the darkness, brought me to a place of deeper awareness of the Light within me, the place inside that is my true self, held eternally in the luminous embrace of God. But of course it wasn't an easy, or simple, or pleasant process, and there were times when

---

1 O'Donohue, John. *Beauty: The Invisible Embrace.* New York: HarperCollins, 2004. 2. Print.

the falling into the ever deeper darkness was so terrifying that I wanted to make it all stop. I didn't really <u>know</u> that it would end, where it would end, where or when or if I would hit bottom. However, somehow I felt the call and the freedom to be true to where I was, to surrender, and through the act of surrender to trust that awakening might unfold as well. To be fully where we are is to surrender and awaken at the same time.

And I could do that—be where I was—because I had people, like you, inviting me to do so, giving me the freedom to not force or fake anything, but simply to be.

"As long as you run from where you are and distract yourself, you cannot fully let yourself be healed. A seed only flourishes by staying in the ground in which it was sown. When you keep digging up the seed to check whether it is growing, it will never bear fruit. Think of yourself as a little seed planted in rich soil. All you have to do is stay there and trust that the soil contains everything you need to grow. This growth takes place even when you do not feel it. Be quiet, acknowledge your powerlessness, and have faith that one day you will know how much you have received."[2]

I love those last lines—they've been my mantra for a while. And now I feel that I do finally know how much I have received—the enormity of God's love allows me to let go of the false control over my life I thought I had and to receive what is freely and abundantly offered me through Christ, whose amazing love redeems all things, even the painful, the terrible, the disappointing. But this is a Truth hard to hold, and we live in the 'not yet' where God's redemption is breaking through the darkness of this world, yet the glory of His Fullness has not been realized just yet.

Truth doesn't seem to be something we get to own. We are so used to possessing things in our culture. We are taught to grasp at things we want, to hoard up for ourselves treasures. But Truth and Beauty cannot be possessed. They are too big and real for the smallness of our grasping. When we try to hold onto them, we close our hands on such a small portion of what they are that it is no longer whole and only but a crumb or tiny speck of what

2 Nouwen, Henri J. M. The Inner Voice of Love: A Journey through Anguish to Freedom. New York: Doubleday, 1996. 31. Print.

really is. It is like trying to own the ocean by filling our pail with water. Or like trying to possess the beach with a handful of sand. So much is lost in the urgency to possess. Truth and Beauty are meant to be enjoyed, received, welcomed. We slip into their depths and experience just part of the whole at any given time. We rest in their rhythms knowing that as one small part slips away from us in the tides of time, another will come flooding in, and all the while we are held in the grander reality of the whole, of which we are intimately a part.

Dear friend, this letter has turned into a very introspective and philosophical treatise. That wasn't my intent when I sat down to write! You are a person who calls forth the deep and true within me, so I guess that's where this comes from. How good to have a friend who brings more and more Beauty to light, who is able to simply be with what is, to welcome life in all its rich and perplexing shades and not force premature or false change. I am so thankful for you and for our friendship, which is something uniquely its own, part me, part you, but fully itself.

As you tiptoe around the edges of your own darkness, know that you are not alone. There is plenty of space for you to be where you are—truly and authentically, even if where you are is standing on the edge—you do not have to plunge into the abyss before you are ready. You do not have to force growth or change. And truly you can't. I stand with you on the edge, and when you are ready to fall inside, I will be there too. I know you have lots of people who love you and can help you carry some of the burden with you. I am certainly one of them. The beautiful thing, which you helped to teach me, is that darkness too can be a gift to others.

I love you, dear friend. I pray that you find peace and comfort in the embrace of God. I look forward to seeing you soon.

Much love,

Stephanie

I folded the letter, opened my journal, and wrote a poem. It was one of those rare poems that just arrives, complete, fully-packaged, and all I had to do was write it down as it flowed out of me: "I cling to the rock/ gripping with all my strength," it began. I shared my poem with Michelle that week, couched in all kinds of clarifications about how I still felt guilty and afraid, but how I was so thankful for this revelation that I still didn't quite understand about God and myself. I told her I was not finished with this processing yet.

Michelle told me there is no end to this. One small revelation leads to another. We do not have the stamina to absorb the impact of God's love all at once; God gives it to us in tiny pieces we can absorb, because that is the most loving thing God can do. She said, "It sounds like you're saying that, in all of this, whether or not Everett needs another surgery, in spite of all of your guilt and anger, you believe God loves you and is near."

Shocked at the truth of the matter put so simply, at the transformation this meant I'd been through in the last two years, I said, "Yes, I think I do."

It was enough. There would be time and space for the next revelation. I didn't need to contrive it or force it, just to be faithful in the practices I'd found that made space for God's voice, and to trust God to speak when it was time. I would make space for God, and I would be borne. God didn't give me what I wanted—Everett's healing without a second surgery—but gave me *enough*: the knowledge that I was loved and God was near. This was something that, even in the happiest of seasons, I had struggled to believe. Now it was engraved on my heart. The truth of it carried me.

REPRIEVE

THE HUMMINGBIRD

To be so small
that all sustenance
comes from beauty itself—
the brightest flowers
under the blue sky.

"Quickly, quickly!
We must catch all we can
before the day passes,
for we are not given many."

I drove again the gray ribbon of freeway between my home and Sister Margaret's. I was grateful for God's revelation, but I was also worn. I brought with me this new trust in God's love, but also my lingering guilt, the guilt that still, deep down, was consuming me, the guilt I didn't understand. Its weight was heavy and I was weary. What would it look like to let go?

We sat out under the broad trees in lawn chairs. I told Sister Margaret of the guilt I carried. I told her how much I feared that I wasn't enough, that I had hurt my son, how sick I felt in my soul.

"It isn't real," she said. "Guilt is what we feel when we act against love, against God, and you have not done that in this."

It isn't real. I wrote her words in my journal, capturing their truth.

"Feel lots of things," she told me. "Feel anxiety, feel empathy. But give Jesus the guilt-like feelings, because they are an illusion."

This was not a load I was ever meant to carry.

I didn't have to carry Everett's suffering, she told me, because Jesus has already carried our suffering. He was carrying me.

With her words, she freed me. She broke the illusion that this was my fault. I no longer had to punish myself for the suffering of my child.

It seems simple, maybe even trite, but it is true: The naming of my guilt as an illusion set me free. The lie was exposed. That false guilt lost its power over me; each time it tried to re-surface I saw through its façade. Whenever guilt crept in, I said to it: "You are not real. You have no power here," and it faded away.

***Invitation to Practice:*
Laying Down our Burdens
How do we let go of the things that weigh upon us?
See p. 211

Days later, Dave, Everett, and I left for Belize with several of our friends. It was an interlude, putting some distance between us and Everett's next surgery. Newly freed from my false guilt, I was ready to step away from the burden of waiting for it for a while.

There were ten of us traveling together, including Stephanie. We were an eclectic group, to say the least—two ten-month-old babies with their parents and grandmas, plus several twenty- and thirty-somethings. Dave and I had planned the trip as our family vacation and invited everyone we knew to come with us. It was a happy entourage.

We spent a week on an island in the Caribbean. The island was made up of one town with three roads, suitable only for bikes, pedestrians, and golf carts. We snorkeled, ate at the local bakery, and played with the babies in the sand.

Dave and I biked to dinner one night. We sat in a restaurant near the water, peering out through the protective plastic sheeting at the birds landing on the pier. We had been married for seven years, and had walked through so much life together. We had become—without realizing it—adults. That night, I looked at Dave, this familiar being so wrapped up in my life that I almost didn't recognize him as separate from myself. His eyes reminded me of the ocean in their ever-changing color.

The next evening, we chartered a small sailboat to take us out for a sunset ride. We circumnavigated the island as the sun sank, listening to stories of the captain's family and the history of the island, and passed around cups of punch and bowls of ceviche.

The sun went quietly to bed, slipping behind a thin blanket of pink cloud. More clouds gathered as the sky darkened. Everett, snuggled against my chest, lifted his sleepy head and looked up toward the top of the sail above us. There he saw the moon, glowing steadily through the soft gray clouds. He reached his little hand up toward the moon and said, "unh! unh!" his baby language for, "Look, Mama! Look!" He had just seen the moon for the first time, and he wanted me to see it, too—this sweet beacon in the cooling night. He was not afraid of the dark.

More clouds gathered, and it began to rain. I covered Everett with a thin blanket. I wrapped my arms around him and he cried a little, ready for sleep. I gripped the boat with one hand as it rolled on the water. I laid my cheek on his head, and sang softly. Slowly he quieted into sleep against my chest, wrapped warm against the wind and the misty rain. Dave stood near, then wrapped his arms around mine as I held our sleeping boy.

We are so blessed.

On our last night on the island, I went to dinner with Stephanie. As we sat together, we marveled. *Look how far we've come,* we said. Stephanie had walked through her grief over infertility to a place of freedom and openness—a wide, lovely meadow of possibility and rest. I had been freed from my false guilt over Everett's surgery and was beginning to trust in God's love.

Look how far we've come, we said. We thanked each other.

We are friends who sit with each other in our pain and sorrow longer than is comfortable or convenient. We walk dark roads together, comforting each other in the shadowy places. We remind each other of God.

We each hope for the other when hope for ourselves is no longer possible. Together, we are brave.

We lingered over dinner, then walked up the beach by moonlight, drinking in the warm ocean breeze. We paused on the beach and hugged each other, watching the palm trees dance in front of the moon, listening to the quiet waves lapping on the shore.

"There is too much beauty here to take in," I said.

"And here we are, part of it all," she replied.

Stephanie's friendship was a beacon in my lost places. Consistently, through infertility and pregnancy and motherhood and Everett's surgery, she led me back to God. She led me back to my own soul. She named things in me I was unable to name, and I did the same for her. Here, we paused to celebrate that together. We said thank you, to God and to each other. We said thank you for this reprieve. We said thank you for this friendship, forged in the fires of our suffering.

On our last morning on the island, we snorkeled. Everett stayed at the cabana with Dave's mom. We were the only boat on the reef. Dark clouds hung over the island in the distance and in the open ocean to the East. We were lit up by sunshine.

I jumped into the chest-deep water. I put my head under, immersed in the watery landscape. All earth-sounds were muted, silenced. Dave and I swam together, holding hands in this underwater playground, following rays and harmless nurse sharks.

We circled back to the boat where our guide had followed us into the water. He was gentle with the sea creatures, and they came to him. Dave and I stopped a few feet away, heads in the water. I felt something brush up behind me, then nuzzle into my hair. I turned to see a nurse shark, puppy-like, begging for a snuggle. As I turned to see the shark untangle itself and swim slowly away, a stingray came up on my other side, brushing against my arm and body. Rays are some of my favorite creatures, so unique in their shape, dangerous but gentle, and softer than velvet. These creatures of the sea were inviting us into their dance.

For the next half hour, we played with this underwater world. Our guide led us. He was patient with the creatures, letting them show him when they wanted to play. There was no exercise of power, only gentle submission to the power of the ocean and the delight of play together.

Thank you, I prayed. *Thank you, thank you, thank you.* Dave and I grinned at each other behind our snorkel masks.

It was time to go. I let my fingertips brush against one last ray, then climbed into the boat. The sun warmed my salty skin, and I peeled off my goggles and flippers. I looked out over the turquoise water and sighed, unable to speak. I looked at Stephanie. "That was magical," I said.

"It was spiritual," she said. "It makes me want to cry."

Still, sometimes, on the most chaotic of my days, when I sit in stillness I reenter those waters. I imagine myself diving in, submerging, all sounds of the dry world shut out by the muffling of the water, the occasional splash of a flipper, and the tiny clicks and whirs of fish feeding in coral. Ocean creatures, in places like Belize, are unafraid. Most wild creatures on land run from the sight of a human, but creatures of the deep welcome us as strange, awkwardly aquatic creatures. They invite us in, knowing, perhaps, that we cannot linger forever. The ocean is a foreign place—massive, dangerous, alluring, and yet gentle, joyful, and playful. On its waves I am borne.

The ocean reminds me how small I am, and yet, when I enter it, I become part of it. It holds me, caresses me, lets me float on its waters or propel myself through them. It shows me how to let go. It is alive—changeable in temperament, breathing in and out, up and down, rolling us in its tumbling waves. It roars loud and laps quiet. It is immense, uncharted, unfathomable. It encompasses our whole world. It humbles me, quiets me, upholds me, and gives me hope in my very smallness before something so great.

I needed this reminder as the summer ended and Everett's surgery crept nearer. I had come far on the road through disillusion, but there was still uncertainty. Still the second surgery loomed, though I prayed we would be spared. The way snaked forward, and I could not see the end, but I was beginning to believe that the One walking with me could be trusted.

RAGE, REST, RELEASE

AUTUMN
The heart sinks
dying
an awful winter
How I wish all this could be spared

Life because death because life
an eternal night
now lies at the bottom

Lost

He gave them morning
a pattern of the world immortal

God has become the center
in the light of the setting sun

ONE DAY, late in August, Everett gave me a rock. It was small and gray and not very interesting, but it was the very first thing he had picked up with intention and brought as a gift for his mama. I carried it around in my pocket for days. Then I wrapped it up in a piece of paper with the date and put it in my desk with the words "from Everett" on it, tucked in the drawer with a few locks of hair from his first trim.

One year before, we had prayed that the baby stay in my womb through August, and he had. This year, I was praying again. I was praying that God would heal Everett, that he wouldn't need another surgery. Every day I hoped that something had changed, that he and we would be spared. Nothing changed.

Anger grew hot in my belly. Anger scares me. It feels out of control, and I like to be in control. Anger is passionate, wild. It seems like it might be hard to rein in once given its head. So I held tightly to the reins.

I went to Sister Margaret. "Give God your anger," she said. "Like you would look on a dirty rock Everett gave to you as a precious gift, God looks on your anger as a gift."

I had not told her about my rock from Everett.

She told me that when I give God my anger, God thinks, "This is how much she loves me. Look what she gave me!" God can make anything beautiful.

And so I prayed. *God, please open my eyes to my own anger. Help me not to be afraid of it.* I let go of the reigns and allowed myself to rage. I rode surges of anger for many months to come and learned that they do pass. I didn't need to be afraid. Doesn't God also rage on behalf of the suffering? My prayers blazed.

I cried in the night. I pictured the surgery perfectly: the "tired tiger" scrubs, the rooms where we'd wait, the awful hallway where we'd lay him down and they'd roll him away. I pictured it in the night, and shuddered, and cried, and cried out—*Save us, God! Save us from this!* I screamed silent screams into my pillow, not wanting to wake Dave. I let out my anger in fits and starts and wrestled with the desperate hope that we would yet be spared. I begged and pleaded, prayers in the night of *please, please, please,* saturated with tears. I dreamed horrible dreams and screamed myself awake.

> **Invitation to Practice:**
> **The Feelings Closet, Reprise**
> What does it look like to lament?
> *See p. 213*

I prayed honest angry prayers and trusted that they were an act of love. As the surgery crept closer with the shortening days, I laid to rest my hope for healing without it. This would be our road. I must learn to walk it well.

As my hope receded, so did my rage. I shifted my focus, trying to enjoy the early fall with Everett before we were in crisis mode once again.

On October 5, Everett turned one, and we celebrated. Four days later, he took his first step. I could see it on his face beforehand, as he stood next to a chair. He let go of the chair he was holding, his face spread into a grin and he toddled forward.

Everett's surgery was scheduled for October 24, and we took a quick trip to the San Francisco Bay Area beforehand. Dave had a class in the city, and Everett and I drove to my aunt's home in Santa Rosa.

I let myself in her front door, carrying Everett in one arm and my first load of bags in the other. I was worn thin from traveling with a baby. My aunt and uncle were out of town until the next day, which gave us a quiet night to ourselves. We played for a while upstairs, and then I put Everett to bed. He went down easily, and I was grateful. Then, in moment of instinct I decided to follow, I spent the evening nurturing and nourishing myself.

I put on my pajamas and I poured a glass of chardonnay. The kitchen was brightly lit against the quickly-darkening sky. I heated sauce, chopped vegetables, and raided the cupboard for oil and vinegar. I boiled gnocchi, scooping it out of the hot water as it floated to the surface. I didn't put on music—the simmering and sizzling and chopping against the silence of the evening and the rhythm of my breath were enough.

Invitation to Practice: Cultivate Gratitude

How do we grow our awareness of the goodness in our lives?

See p. 215

I sat at the table with my journal closed, sipped chardonnay and ate the gnocchi, piping hot. It filled my belly and my soul, nourishing and nurturing. I was content. What a messy, rich life I have been given. In that moment, God said to me, in the quiet, not-quite-audible voice I was coming to recognize, *[See? I will take care of you. Life won't be like this, but there will always be moments like this.]*

I invited God to sit with me, and God came. *[I love you,]* God said, in the warmth that filled me. *[I love you, and I will take care of you.]* We sat together, I was fed, and I was grateful.

The LORD is my shepherd; I prayed. *I shall not want. He makes me lie down in green pastures; he leads me beside still waters. He restores my soul.*[1]

That night God restored me through my own two hands. I cared for myself the way I would care for another at the end of an exhausting week, and God met me. I rested.

---

1 Psalm 23:1-3

Today was one of the hardest days, I wrote in my journal on October 23, the day before Everett's scheduled surgery, when we found out we'd have to delay the surgery because he was sick with a cold. We didn't know when he'd be well enough to reschedule.

Our best-laid plans were thrown up in the air. The out-of-town guests scheduled to fly in and help would no longer be perfectly timed. We would have to reschedule the dozen people bringing us meals. We may no longer be the first surgery of the day, the easiest time for little guys like Everett.

I didn't get to control this. Not even a little bit.

I raged once again.

That night, Everett woke again and again in his sickness, coughing and crying. I woke, again and again, to stumble downstairs in my heavy-lidded exhaustion to nurse him back to sleep. By morning, I saw myself in a broken pile at the feet of God. *That's it,* I said. *You win. I am broken. I have nothing left.*

I floated through the day in a dark mist. I gave God my anger: *Why must we go through this surgery? Why, if we must, must it be like this?* I could not hear an answer. Where was the God I thought I knew?

I remembered the vision I'd had, nine months before, of Everett running free in a field and God, as a red-tailed hawk, watching over him. I held my hands open to God, asking God to be worthy of my trust, as I know God is. I began to believe I was borne, even in this.

As each day went by and we waited for health, I had enough—just barely, but enough—to get through and not be consumed. A friend came by to take Everett for a walk, enough to get me through that day. I painted a crazy picture I didn't understand but somehow spoke my feelings. It was enough for another day. Our housemates played with Everett in the yard. They gave me time to vacuum the house.

Slowly, I surrendered to trust. Surgery would happen when it happened. For now, we could rest and eat dinner in bed and take long walks with Everett. We could enjoy these free days.

One day I knew there was something I had to do. I made an appointment.

———❖———

I brought Stephanie with me. We walked under the neon lights and through the glass door, in from the cool night. She waited at a distance, pondering the images on the walls. I headed to the back and laid my wrist before the artist.

Slowly, painfully, an image unfolded: a red-tailed hawk in flight.

———❖———

One week later, I sat in a teashop. My skin was healing, the injured layer peeling off to reveal new color below. I pondered a question from Stephanie: "Autumn is a season of release. What are you being asked to let go of?"

I thought about Everett, and his surgery, now scheduled for the next day. I was being asked to let go of control—control over Everett's life, his safety, his comfort, health, and happiness. I wanted to shape his journey—from his schedule and diet to the way people talked to

Invitation to Practice: Embracing Seasons

How do we live into the season in which we find ourselves?

See p. 217

See p. 217

him and the things that did or didn't happen in his life. I carried the weighty responsibility of his whole life on my own insufficient shoulders. But I am not enough for Everett. In tender contrast to my realization in his early life that I *was* enough—enough mother, enough to satisfy his needs—I now realized that I was also not enough.

What a lovely paradox! We are enough and not enough at the same time. That is the story of the Christian life. I am enough: made in God's image, redeemed by Jesus, beloved and being made perfect. I am also not enough, and I am not asked to be. I am part of a beautiful whole: me + God + the people around me = a living, vibrant, diverse, and unified body, the body of Jesus. I am only a part.

The life I imagined for Everett, one I carefully controlled, was less vibrant and colorful and *good* than a life shaped by God in partnership with the many loving, creative, kind people in his life. To let go of my control would be to let go of a responsibility I couldn't carry anyway, and to release Everett into the freedom he would find in God's great hands, instead of clasped too tightly in my finite ones. I did not need to bear Everett's life as my burden; he was already borne, as was I. I must allow him to be shaped by his pain, just as I had been shaped by mine.

[Be free, small one,] God said.

Today, I look to the ink on my skin as a reminder of what I want to believe. This is what I remember:

God spoke to me. When I felt alone, abandoned, and unworthy, when I feared I had forsaken my son as he awoke from surgery—his time of greatest need—God sent me a vision of a hawk, God's own self flying high over Everett, taking in all the details of Everett's life with powerful raptor vision. God sees the intimate details of our lives, like a hawk sees a tiny mouse moving under grass. God is watching over Everett when I can't. God is also watching over me.

There are more layers of meaning to this symbol. The cry of the red-tailed hawk pierces the soul with its pure animal joy—the sound of freedom, of effortless flight. I remember first hearing their cries with my dad, as we sat on the cliffs above the river at my grandparents' farm. That brings me to another layer: Somewhere deep down, hawks are a reminder of where I come from, of family, of home.

Why the wrist? Each time I see it, it is a reminder to keep my hands open, to let go and to receive whatever it is God has for me. It marks me where Christ was marked for me.My hawk is a sign of the already-not-yet kingdom; a symbol of who I was, who I am, and who I hope to be; a picture of what I've learned and what I hope to remember. One day, when it is a bit more creased and faded, it will remind me to let Everett leave the nest. At the last, may it remind me of the unfettered joy to which I fly.

LULLABY

WHERE WERE YOU?
You broke me
completely
and yet I love you still.

Why is that?

I seek you, still,
though I thought you walked away
when I needed you most.

Why?

"Relent, relent!" I called——
release us from this hell!
——and yet I love you still.

Why?

Because you were there, too,
and you didn't walk away.

Because you, too, were broken
over the broken body of your beloved Son——
and you declared this beautiful.

You walked toward, instead of away.

You are persistent, gracious, patient, kind;
you are large, abundant, unfathomable——

and yet you see me still.

You love enough to write in me this story
and you wait for me, in all my anger, to return——

and you call it trust.

THIS IS HELL.

Everett won't stop screaming and writhing. I'm on hold with Children's Hospital. God help us. I don't know what to do.

I hold him.

I get through to the hospital, only to be told there is nothing else they can do for his pain. How can this be?

At last, Everett falls asleep in my arms. Too soon, he awakens, screaming.

The LORD is my strength. I cannot protect him, I can only comfort.

This night is endless.

Everett cries; he will cry forever. Surgery is over—it worked—but why does he scream? I cannot stop it. God, you are breaking us.

We keep going not because we are strong or persevering or faithful but because we have no choice. What is this, some kind of desperate, angry trust?

I am utterly powerless to stop the pain.

Dave and I take turns holding Everett while he screams. My mom brings me a glass of water.

I hold him and he screams. I sing over him. I cry out, *fix this! Show up, now!*

All I can do is hold him in his pain, just as God holds me in mine.

It is morning.

Two days later my mom gets on a plane back to Wisconsin. I want to beg her to stay but I don't. She would, but she shouldn't. There is nothing she can do to make this better. There is nothing I can do to make this better. How we ache for our children.

Everett's pain ebbs. Friends bring meals and groceries. Housemates come to sit with us quietly. Dawn begins to break.

Then everything falls apart.

Everett's bandage falls off early. His medical equipment falls out of place. I call the hospital. I call again. I demand attention. I fight for my son. What went wrong last time is happening again and I am the only one who sees. Only I can stop it. But I can't stop it.

We go to the hospital. They do what they can; it isn't much.

Will we be doomed to this yet again?

I want to pray, but I have no words. I find the words of others.

Hear my prayer, O Lord, and give ear to my cry; do not be silent at my tears.[1]

O Lord, listen! Hear and act![2]

I sing lullabies to my beloved son.

Everett wakes screaming in the night, and I imagine his nightmares.

Relent, I pray. *Relent!*

Dave's mom arrives. She takes Everett for walks and helps around the house. Dawn begins to break.

But the equipment slips again and we run to the ER in the night, and we wait and show Everett diggers on the TV above the hospital bed, and we pray *help!* and the nurses come, and no one seems to know what they are doing and my baby is crying and I hold him hard and he hurts! he hurts! and I am numb beyond all tears. And the doctor comes and he is kind. He does what needs to be done and we go home to rest.

The dawn breaks but I cannot see. Everett wakes happy. He smiles and walks and dances. His body is starting to heal. Lord, have mercy. Let this be the end.

I have tea with Stephanie. I recount the days since the surgery. I feel only numb. Each time I think the worst has passed something else falls apart.

"What does it mean that God is faithful?" I ask. "What does it mean when things don't work out OK in the end?" This I ask my friend whose womb is still empty, and yet she believes.

---

1 Psalm 39:12

2 Daniel 9:19

"Maybe you don't have to ask those questions right now. The storm has not yet passed, and already you assess the damage. Just be kind to yourself, day by day."

————— ❊ —————

Everett is asleep downstairs and Dave is at work. I fall to my knees on our bedroom floor. *Why?!* I yell aloud at God, and I slam my fists into the carpet. *Why?!* I hold my knees to my chest and I rock and cry and choke on my tears, cover my face with my hands, scream into my palms. My hair hangs in salty clumps. I curl on the floor, smell weeks of accumulated dust. *Why?* I beat my fists on the carpet. *Why?* I beat the chest of this God I'd thought was holding me so close. *Where were you? Where are you? Why did you let this happen?*

I choke on my tears and blow my nose and make a mound of Kleenex on the floor. I clench my fists and scream into my knuckles and rock back and forth and back again. I am shattered.

It passes.

I am grateful for grief. But still, I am full of unshed tears. There is not time enough to shed them all.

> **Invitation to Practice: Reflections on Trust**
>
> What does trusting God look like when everything falls apart?
>
> *See p. 219*

I blow my nose one last time and I watch some bad TV. I go to dinner with a friend and eat dumplings and green beans from Din Tai Fung. The next day, I vacuum.

————— ❊ —————

Everett heals, slowly. It will be months before I stop worrying, but our final trip to the ER seems to have done the trick. Our little boy will be OK.

I go to Sister Margaret. It is Advent. I haven't noticed.

"Walk with Mary through Advent," she says. "Let her sing through you, let her hold your child with you, let her sorrow with you in his pain."

Advent is a time of darkness before dawn, she says. Joy is hidden like the sun during rain, but after the rain, it's glorious. As we go through darkness, the light is there, and the darkness itself helps us see the dawn. God meets us there in the darkness and walks with us through it. God comes after us and goes before us.

Sister Margaret prays for tears.

I walk through Advent's darkening days, and I wait. I don't know what I want. I don't want to think, don't want to feel, and yet I want to feel and cry and move on. I want to sleep and sleep. The earth and I have moved from fall's release to winter's darkness.

One day, I draw a cluster of snow-covered trees in my journal. Next to them, I write: *Like a still, silent, snow-covered forest, I wait.*

I talk about Advent with women I love as we sit together on my bed in the cold winter evenings. I share pots of tea with Stephanie. I read Rainer Maria Rilke, and hold the hope in his grasping, struggling, I-don't-understand-but-I'm-in-love-with-the-mystery poems. *But you take pleasure in the faces/of those who know they thirst/You cherish those/who grip you for survival.*[3] I imagine Mary as we wait for Christmas. I sit in dark forests in my mind, naked before God, waiting. I wait with kindness for my broken, mending self.

One night in December, Stephanie comes and we take Everett for a walk. We wander our neighborhood, then climb to the top of Barnsdall Park. As we crest the hill, the sun is setting over a shockingly clear view of the blue-green ocean, far across the vastness of Los Angeles. I stand with this deep soul-friend of mine, and we talk about God's will, and how it's not some magic plan for us to follow into the future, but it is here, and it is now. God's will is not a cryptic map for life we are supposed to decipher. Following God's will is about attentiveness and acceptance. Most

3 Rilke, Rainer Maria. Rilke's Book of Hours: Love Poems to God. Trans. Anita Barrows and Joanna Macy. New York: Riverhead, 1996. 71. Print.

often, God shows up in the interruptions to our plans; those interruptions break the illusion that we were ever in control. That is when we find rest in hands much greater than our own.

We stand on the hill together, and I squeeze her hand. I am present to the cooling breeze and the darkening day and this knowledge that God is here, and God is now. God knows, and I do not have to. In time, this, too, will be made beautiful, even if I never see it. I need only to accept, and to wait with kindness.

III. BLESSED IN HOPE

Trust in the LORD and do good;
dwell in the land and enjoy safe pasture.
Take delight in the LORD,
and he will give you the desires of your heart.
Psalm 37: 3-4

(DIS)CONTENT

THERE WILL EVER BE ENOUGH

If, one day, I lose my family,
I will yet have this dear friend
to walk with me toward you.
And if she, too, is lost
I will seek another,
for there must be others
to be sought.
And if all living are no more
I will seek solace
among the dead—I will bring
my books to the woods
and find you there.
And if
all books are ash
all trees
are books
are ash
there will be sky
where I can find you.
And if, while I yet walk,
the sky is beyond
all imagination dead
yet still
there will
be
you.

WHEN DAVE AND I moved to California for his graduate school, we had planned to stay for three years, then move back to the Midwest. To me "Midwest" meant Madison, where I grew up. It meant home. When we were first married, I was all for an adventure on the West coast. We would enjoy our early marriage in a new place, then we'd move home and start a family.

By the time Dave finished graduate school, I was working a job I loved and we were part of the Kairos church family; it would be hard to leave. "One more year," we said. One became three, and then Everett was born. That year his surgeries dominated our attention. As he healed and the year waned, I became restless.

As Everett grew, I longed to be close to family so they could watch him grow. I wanted Everett to know his family deeply, and moving back to Wisconsin seemed the simplest way to ensure that kind of knowing.

I imagined Friday mornings with my mom. We'd have a cup of tea together. Then she would take Everett to the park while I sat on her porch and wrote. I imagined sleepovers with Everett's cousins; they would grow up together. I imagined cross country skiing through the woods in winter, then warming ourselves by the fireplace in my parents' living room, the same hearth that warmed me as a child. I pictured a childhood for Everett very like my own, but with a proximity to extended family I never had. I mourned the loss of the time we'd been away since he was born. Perhaps, I also mourned the loss of my own childhood.

Dave's schedule also motivated us to find something new. He was working full time at his graduate school, part time as a pastor at Kairos, and also getting his doctorate. He is a high-capacity person, and he loved what he was doing, but we knew this wasn't sustainable. Even if we were to stay in Los Angeles, something would have to change for us to live the kind of life we sought: an integrated life, in which there was overlap between vocation and family; a life in which we lived near where we worked and played. We started to ask God a question: "Is Los Angeles our forever place?"

I didn't want it to be. Especially in the blistering heat of summer, I had a hard time with Los Angeles. I don't belong in California. Sunshine is overrated. I belong in a land of lush forests, fresh water, and thunderstorms.

When I closed my eyes at a Kairos gathering one night, I saw our family nestled in the palm of a great hand, high above a sparkling city. What did it mean? Would God lift us out of Los Angeles one day?

I was ready to be released from Los Angeles. Yet, at the same time, I wanted to be rooted where we were. I wanted to love our neighborhood, and that was a love I would have to work hard to cultivate.

I told God about my discontent. I asked God questions and listened for answers in my art: *Where am I closing my eyes to wonder? How can you help me to find more peace?* Asking questions was an act of surrender. I was turning control of my present and my future to God. I painted and collaged—images of cityscapes and deep roots, flying birds and door handles. I visited my art again and again, looking for clues as to what God was saying. In this, I learned a new way to listen. I saw in these images my paradoxical desires to take root and take flight, and wondered whether or not a door would open to lead us out of Los Angeles. *I want to go home*, I prayed. God asked, [*But will you follow me anywhere?*]

Invitation to Practice: Beauty Walk

How do we cultivate an awareness of the beauty around us?

See p. 222

The intensity of my desire to move home to Wisconsin kept Dave and me up late in the night talking. I felt guilty about my desire, unable to see God's will through the haze of what I wanted. "Watch for signs of beauty," Dave told me. "We live an enviable life." Though it wasn't the life I had hoped for, I knew Dave was right. I took his advice.

We walked. Everett and I ventured outside of our urban oasis daily to explore. Sometimes we stopped at Barnsdall Park, where Everett played peek-a-boo among the columns or toddled after dogs in the grass. The view, always, was incredible. After rain, we could see the ocean. We played with Everett's baby friends, two of them born within a few weeks of Everett and living just blocks away. We hunted for treasures at Goodwill. We ate hand-rolled tortillas at our favorite taco shop, Everett sitting up on the long counter. At every turn, I was blessed.

And yet, the dark side to this neighborhood was also evident: condoms and pornography and broken vodka bottles. There was a man who had been living on our corner for six months. He was usually horizontal, bare-chested, bottle propped at his mouth. There was a permanent stain on the sidewalk where his urine ran into the gutter. Whether we said hello or not, he was unresponsive. I did not know his name.

I saw domestic battles among the people who lived outside in the park: yelling, swearing, posturing, and very-near-but-not-quite violence.

With two attempted assaults and two fatal shootings in our neighborhood within a few weeks, the sound of hovering helicopters made me afraid to go outside.

There was a dirt patch in the sidewalk we passed every day that looked like it was intended for a tree or plants. Instead, it was bare, sooty dirt, littered with adult classifieds, an empty cigarette pack, and a couple of dirty napkins. One day I noticed a little bit of green popping up through the cracked surface. Soon, it was more than a little bit of green. In a few weeks, it was a daffodil.

Beauty endures. Everywhere, it endures. On good days, I see the beauty. On bad days, I see the mess. On my best days, I see both, and hold them together in my mind like one tightly woven fabric. I learned to do the same with my contentment and discontent. I could love where I was and hope for change at the same time.

One day I walked by that dirt patch, and it was made new: Someone had picked up the garbage, left the no-longer-blooming-but-still-green daffodil, and filled in the patch with smooth, gray stones. Someone, I don't know who, cared enough to make this place a little bit better.

I love Los Angeles because the city *needs*. It's a crazy mix of rich and poor, have-it-alls and want-to-get-its, one of the most ethnically diverse cities in the world. The longer I lived there, the more I saw how this city paralleled my own life: I, too, am made up of both great beauty and great pain, which knit together to create my very self. When there was darkness in my heart, beauty still sprang forth, and when I paid attention, I could cultivate it. I didn't have to be joyful or sad or angry—I could be all three at the same time. Most of us are.

Once upon a time, I came home from each vacation with a sinking feeling in my belly: I saw the smog and the desert and the concrete. Then I learned to see the sparkling city lights and the people who live by them.

As Dave and I continued our conversations about what might be next, I put effort into growing deep roots. It would be more painful to pull them up, I knew, if and when the time came to leave, but it would be worth it. I can't live well without a sense of belonging.

I held my hope for change and my growing love for this place in tension. I waited.

AT THE THRESHOLD

LINGER

I stand at the threshold——
the place both
everywhere and
no-where—
on the border of the here and now
and always.
I stand at the threshold
and wait,
and then the air moves—
we meet again.
You, who meet me beyond all knowing
in the in-betweens:
between sleeping and waking
between searching and finding
in the mysterious always that is never now and ever
here
in dawn, dusk, and the fall of a dying leaf.
The air moves, and you are here——
One beyond all——
One above, below, behind, before, and through—
through whom I see, I am.
You meet me here——
at the threshold——
and I wait for you.
I hear your whispers on the wind,
an invitation to become.

WAKEN me.

This became my prayer as I walked the line between hope and contentment. I wanted a different life in a new place. This I knew, but I also really, truly, loved the life we had. I wanted to awaken to the blessings in front of me.

With the start of the new year, Dave looked for a new job, mostly within a few hours of our families. We had come to the conclusion that, though our lives are not wrapped around his career, a job shift was the most natural starting point for our family to build a new life. I prayed for our future, often—that God would reveal where we were to go and what we were to do, and that God's imagination for it would be bigger than anything we dared hope. I prayed for unity and clarity for Dave and me. I also prayed for the present—that I would find new ways to put down roots in Los Angeles, and that I would discover what unique gifts I had to share with those I loved in this season of our life. I knew that if I didn't actively cultivate contentment where I was, I would never find it anywhere. Here, now, is all we have. I prayed for peace.

One day, I led a group of women from Kairos in an artistic listening exercise adapted from *The Artist's Rule* by Christine Valters Paintner.[1] On note cards, we asked God three questions and listened for answers through art. We asked about the past, present, and future. For the future, I asked God how we would know what to do, with the footnote "I am afraid." The collage that serendipitously ended up on the back of the card contained a cartoon of a man pulling on a door handle, then running into the door, because it was locked. [*Start trying doors, and see if they're open,*] I heard.

With contentment, I waited for an open door.

One day months later I was on the front porch when Dave arrived home from work.

"I found a job posting that looks intriguing," he said. He paused. We were standing in the doorway. "It's in the Bay Area. So I don't need to apply for it." He hesitated in deference to my desire.

"Tell me about it," I said.

"Well, the church looks really cool. I just stumbled across the website, and it seems really similar to Kairos. Then I noticed their job posting."

1   Paintner, Christine Valters. *The Artist's Rule: Nurturing Your Creative Soul with Monastic Wisdom.* Notre Dame, IN: Sorin, 2011. 32-34. Print.

"What's the job?"

He described something very similar to the "dream job" we had discussed months earlier—a job that, in months of searching, he had not found anywhere. "It may not exist," he had told me.

"We don't need hundreds of jobs; we just need one," I had replied.

In this moment on the porch, I remembered the note cards I had created.

"Apply," I told him. "I feel like in this season, God is asking us to keep trying doors to see if they're open."

He looked at me searchingly, a slow grin tugging at the corners of his mouth: "The name of the church is Open Door."

We laughed together at the irony, and deep in my soul, I wondered. We went inside.

One month later, Kairos held a Good Friday service at our house. We read scripture together, shared the Eucharist, and sat in silence together. There were about a dozen friends from Kairos, and Stephanie was with us. Dave encouraged us to enter the darkness of Good Friday.

After the service, Stephanie and I sat on our porch and talked by candlelight. I told her about Open Door, and how I was trying to hold my heart open to whatever might be coming despite my longing to be near family.

We asked each other questions we couldn't answer. *What does it mean to enter the darkness of Good Friday when we know Easter is coming? What does it mean to enter the anguish and pain of the dying, the forsaken son, and the forsaking parent?* We admitted our growing comfort with the story of God, but our greater confusion about what exactly the story of Jesus means. *Why does life require death? Does it really have to be this way? What does atonement even mean?* Dave sat on the porch railing, chatting with us a while. He said that, in part at least, the cross is God demonstrating complete love and forgiveness in and through humankind's most heinous act—the torture and murder of an innocent. And so, there is no question: God's forgiveness, God's grace, is utterly sufficient. That much made sense to me.

We went to bed, and I dreamed of the in-between: of travel, of torture, of Jesus. They were uncomfortable dreams. It was an uncomfortable time; I don't like un-knowing. I awoke the next day to the Great Sabbath, the day of limbo between Good Friday and Easter, between death and new life.

Invitation to Practice: Thresholds

How do we invite God into the threshold spaces in our lives?

See p. 224

We exist in the in-between; that is how we enter the darkness of Good Friday. We live the pain and the anguish and the heartache that are so much of what it means to be human. We are caught: By faith we are beyond death, yet we still await new life. God has promised to make all things new, but all things are not yet new. We are the already-not-yet Kingdom of God, bringing whatever peace, goodness, love, and forgiveness we can to the world. Forever we are trying to find our way back home.

On that Great Sabbath, in the midst of unknown, I rested in in-be-tweenness. In the last three years, my world had been dominated by infertility, then pregnancy and parenthood and surgeries and now this stark-as-blank-white-page future. Heading from hardship to the unknown, my mind was spinning. It was too much for me to process. Would I ever feel settled?

On that day of in-betweens, I printed a picture of the *Pieta* and glued it into my journal. I studied the face of Mary as she held the broken body of her son. What was written there? What was she thinking, what was she feeling as she suffered in the in-between? I knelt on the floor of our bedroom in a quiet moment and I waited with Mary. I remembered the broken, now-healed body of my own beloved son, and I looked upon the body of this Savior of mine in awe.

We have a God who was poured out like water,[2] who suffered through birth and life and death and was laid in the dust. Our God knows what it is to forsake and what it is to be forsaken. God entered the in-between for us.

---

2 Psalm 22

On the Great Sabbath I was at a threshold, pausing to soak in all the nourishment I could from the season in which I lingered, wondering what lay ahead. This truth began to settle on my heart: God is enough. God has to be enough. Nothing else is.

BOARDING A PLANE

CHANNEL ISLANDS
The dry grass piles before my toes
like soft snow

I look to the hills—
the golden invaders
have taken over hill and valley
covering them with light
and you hold me in the palm
of your warm hand

I walk the hills
wade the rushing river of wind and shadow
rolling tumbling rolling tumbling
my shadow is tall
like a mountain
(rolling tumbling
rolling tumbling)
my heart is warm
and wide

We are all grasses bending in the same wind

A voice speaks in the night: "Come."

THE DAYS CONTINUED to lengthen, and I floated between restlessness and contentment. I thought often of my childhood home in Wisconsin as summer approached: of walking in the forest, of canoeing on the lake, of fireflies. I continued to cultivate contentment in Los Angeles, even as I carried within me the hope that our time there was ending.

I wondered about this job Dave had applied for at Open Door. He had a few interviews and came away from each hesitantly excited. The job, the people, and the place were what he wanted, but they weren't what I wanted. He knew that. I asked him questions and listened well, trying to reserve any judgment for the time being. My heart was beginning to tell me this could be real, this could be our future. I didn't want to believe it yet. The Bay Area wasn't our plan, and it wasn't what I wanted. But I was learning to trust God to be especially present in the interruptions to my plans.

Before I knew it, we were boarding a plane.

Dave was more surprised than I that Open Door had invited us up for an interview weekend. The knowledge that this could be real had continued to grow within me. I was calm.

Open Door's worship pastor picked us up at the airport. We drove through the tunnel and the golden hills to Pleasant Hill, where we would stay with a couple from the church, Brendan and Emily.

After putting Everett to bed, we met Brendan and Emily in the living room. Emily was sitting on their comfortable couch, wide enough for four, and Brendan was pouring drinks. An old movie was on in the background. We chatted easily, like old friends, despite the strangeness of unknowing—where would this weekend lead? Were we going to be friends, or would this be an awkward blip on our life-paths? A delicious, almost liquid breeze poured through the open windows. "Do you get breezes like this every night?" I asked.

"Yes, it's pretty normal!"

It smelled green.

The rest of the weekend was a blur of brunches and meetings and naps and walks and dinners. We met dozens of people. Everywhere, we were met with warmth and kindness.

Everett, now one and a half, was remarkably happy. Not only happy—he was independent, far more so than in social gatherings at home in LA. He wandered away from us at a potluck, playing with other kids and exploring. At a pizza place one night, he went around to each table, pointing to person after person and saying, "Fwend! Fwend! Fwend! Fwend!" His experience of this place was unclouded by desire or fear or knowledge of what the weekend might mean. His innocent comfort spoke volumes of the sincerity of these strangers.

Sunday's gathering was about trusting God in the unknown. As we sang together, in my mind's eye I saw again a great hand holding our family above the lights of a city. Tears coursed my cheeks, and I held Dave's hand, and I saw his eyes glistening, too. Our months and years of questions, prayers, hoping, waiting, and planning were culminating in this moment. [Be brave.]

--------❖--------

Two weeks earlier, we are camping in the Channel Islands.

It is Everett's first backpacking trip. We search for the cat-like island foxes in the tall grass and hang our hammock in the trees. We search the beach for interesting rocks. We fly kites.

We hike at sunset, just catching the last rays of the sun as they dip below the horizon. I sing Everett to sleep. He is worn out from a day in the wind and sunshine, and so are we. We sleep well.

In the darkness, well before dawn, I awaken to a word: [Come.] It shimmers in the air of the dark tent around me. I slip as quietly as I can out of my sleeping bag, out of the tent, trying not to wake my sleeping son. The voice calls [Come] and so I follow. I step out into the not-yet dawn and I follow the voice through the dark and up the hill, over the chalky rocks, into the high wind-swept grass. The lingering stars fade as I crest the hill, and I look for the other path, the one along the cliff's edge that I know is there, but I can't find it, so, eventually, I cut up the hillside, carefully treading around clumps of flowers. I find it—the path I have been looking for—not ten yards away. It traces the edge of the cliff, as I knew it would, and the ocean booms and roars below, and I stand at the edge and wait, I know not how long, for the voice of the One to reveal what I am to know. I stand at the edge, and watch, and taste the salt air. I listen to the sea boom and roar and echo and call. I hold my arms wide to the sea and the wind and the rocks and the One and then I wrap them tight around myself, hold my soul in my chest, calm the fluttering butterfly with the firm warmth of my two strong arms. I listen. I wait. I calm. I hear, [Walk with me. Walk with me beyond your fear. I am with you.]

My desire to chase after this God I have come to know, this God who loves, bears, and blesses me, now outweighs the rest. I will follow. I will go.

I close my eyes and open arms wide once again to the wind, but now my soul soars, rides the wind on wings of power, and I am filled and unafraid. I laugh in joy and sing with the wind and with the waves and with the One as the day dawns and the sun breaks over the hills. I dance my delight, and the sun warms my body, and I drop hands to sides and I turn, cut through the grass and down the hill, over the chalky rocks, past the bend in the road, to the place under the trees where my two loves are just waking.

[*Be brave.*] I squeezed Dave's hand and dried my tears, and afterward, I carried within me the ever-growing knowledge that something was coming to fruition.

I awoke the next morning surprised by the certainty that this was something I wanted. On paper, it was not—I wanted to move to Wisconsin, to be near family. But these people had won my heart with their sincerity. We used the same language to talk about Jesus. We asked the same questions.

More than that, I knew deep in my soul that this was right. Here was a place I could belong. I was undone, overwhelmed with desire for something I thought I didn't want to happen. Dave and I were being given the unity for which we had prayed. Dave's and my disparate desires were being transformed into one. In letting go of what I had always wanted, here was this gift.

We went home, and we waited. Just over a week later, I was sitting on the porch while Everett napped, catching up on email. A message from Dave popped up on my computer: "Unanimous yes."

I was overcome with gratitude. I knelt on the floorboards of our porch and cried. This wasn't what I had thought I wanted, but it was *good.* Our waiting was at an end. *Thank you,* I prayed. I wrapped my arms around my chest and felt the beating of my heart.

The door was open.

On June 2, we accepted Open Door's job offer. We had six weeks left in LA.

There was great joy and great loss. I danced around the edges of my grief, trying to distinguish its size and shape. It felt like the edge of an ocean. What did it contain? The loss of these deep relationships, this community we'd cultivated in Los Angeles. The loss of my daily life in the neighborhood I had grown to love. The deeper, harder loss of the elusive dream of mine to move home to Wisconsin. I was grateful, but how was I to give up that dream?

FOR THE FIRST TIME

AND WE SAY YES[1]

In the beginning God created:
God created them,
yes, God created them.

And God said:
"Come, let us go down,"
and the Lord came down.

And God said:
"I will show you,
I will;
I will bless you,
I will,
and you will be a blessing."

God said fill the earth,
fill the whole earth—
and the whole earth
is filled with God's glory—
because God cannot be expressed
in one expression of human beings.

And God said:
"You are the Imago Dei;
see me on display."

You can take it down——
take it to the East,
take it to the North
to the South, to the West—
take the Imago Dei on display.

And everybody was saying yes,
Lord yes, until
it became: I shall
not, I shall not
be moved.

And God said:
"I've got a plan for the whole earth,
not just those who get your jokes."

So you will move.

Now here's what I see:
We have to be careful
where we settle
and what
we settle for;
where you settle
could be where
you die——
because the money ran out,
and the hope ran out.

But no——
you can keep the movement going
if you try.

Will you say yes,
Lord yes?

With my whole-scared-broken heart
I will say:
YES.

God, give us the grace
to do now what we profess.

---

1 Adapted by Kristen Kludt from a teaching by Dr. Brenda Salter McNeil

IT IS NIGHT. We walk down the street holding hands, my heels clicking on the pavement. We laugh as a bus roars by, my skirt ruffling in its wake. Dave races me to the elevator button, and as the metal doors open, we step inside. We go down.

Down, under the pavement, to the land of roaring trains and bright fluorescent lights. We sit together on a concrete bench, slightly giddy with the freedom of being out of the house at night without our baby.

A man shuffles past, dragging a heavy suitcase. A well-dressed woman thumbs at her phone, headphones in her ears.

I hear it before I see it: the hum of a train down the tunnel. Next comes a warm rush of wind. Then comes the light, curving ahead of the train around the bend. Then, in a breath, the train is here, doors open, ready for us. We alight.

We take the train downtown, disembark in another tunnel under another dark street. We turn the wrong way once, circling the block in search of our destination. There it is—I see the right address—and we go inside. Ahead is an elevator, with a tiny metal bird perched next to the number 15.

Up, up, up we go, to the top. We step off, walk through deep red drapery. Beyond are tables, lights, clinking glasses, and the hum of a string quartet. Beyond that, the balcony, the skyline, the night.

The view takes my breath.

This is our city. How is it that as I leave this place I find I am in love with it after all?

I lean against the railing, watching the city as it falls below and rises above me. I am at the top of one of the mid-sized buildings downtown, waist-level to the skyscrapers. Windows light the way above and below, tiny beacons in the night.

Invitation to Practice:
Leaving Well

How do we end a season well?

See p. 226

For the last five years, I have tuned my eyes to see and my ears to hear. I have sat in silence; I have prayed; I have created; I have loved. I have intentionally made space for God to speak.

All at once, I remember these lights. Twice before, in my mind's eye, I have seen a vision: the great hand of God cradling my family far above the sparkling lights of an unknown city. Twice before, I have wondered: What does this mean? Where is this sparkling city? Where is this unknown home I seek?

All at once, I know. All of this has been a search for Home. From the very beginning, when Dave and I were first dreaming of children, it was Home I sought: a family in which I could find myself loved, held, needed. Disappointment crushed that longing, and for two years I lived in that disappointment, learned to find myself at home in it, learned to find myself beloved, even then.

Everett was born, and I had that home, but it wasn't enough. Disillusion took over as I discovered I was not the mother I thought I could be. I was not perfect. I was not strong enough to protect my son. I could not create a home that would save him from harm; I could only give him the tools he needed to travel well.

Finally, hope—I held onto hope in my years of discontent, soaking in the blessings in front of me. I always believed that one day we would move back to Wisconsin, to home. There, in the arms of my extended family, I would find what I was looking for.

But that was not to be. Even that, in the end, would not have been enough. I would arrive only to discover it wasn't the Home I sought.

I see again the vision of being held high above the city lights, and this is what I know now: It is not the unknown sparkling city that is home. It is the hand. Here, safe in the palm of my God, I have been Home all along. The paths I have wandered on this good way through are creases in the palm of my God. The warmth I have felt in the love of another is the warmth of God's skin, God's very blood pulsing beneath the surface. The lights on this dark road are Light itself, emanating from the hand that holds me. All along I have wondered where I belong. I belong in the hand of God.

This is Home. All of this is Home. The sidewalks with the buses roaring by, the trains in the tunnels with the fluorescent lights, the balcony of the skyscraper. The depression that came with infertility. The lostness of motherhood. The cultivating of contentment when what I wanted was somewhere else. These are not my path home; they are Home.

I have sought the good way through, and I have found it in the arms of God. Home is not at the other end of the good way through, it is the good way through. Here, on the Way, I am beloved, I am borne, and I am abundantly blessed. What more could I seek in a Home? What more could I seek in a place to dwell, to love and be loved, to become? We are a pilgrim people, forever wandering and forever home.

---※---

In the weeks following, I see Home everywhere, even as I say good-bye. I spend one last evening with Stephanie, in her home that has become my home. I give her a compass, which she has been for me. She gives me a poem. "When the nights lengthen and shadows linger," it says, "we have this fire of our friendship, which has been so kindled with love that it burns, and dances, and roars, a small fire, radiant in the gathering darkness." She is my hearth, my home-fire, the hands and feet of God. I embrace her one last time.

On our last night at Kairos, this dear community of ours sits with us around a table. After dinner, they tell story after story of our time together. Dave and I hold hands and they pray for us, gathering around us in a half-circle facing the open windows.

I drive to Sister Margaret's through a downpour to spend one last quiet hour in her presence. "In God we live and move and have our being," she tells me. "Looking for God is like a fish looking for the ocean. We don't know where this life will lead us, but God is always with us. Sometimes we are carried, sometimes we are holding hands, but we are not alone—never alone."

It is only now that I understand. God is the Home I have sought, and I am here, all the time.

God, You are everywhere. You are the warmth in a cup of tea, the light on a blade of grass, the wind in the trees. You are the wetness of the tears on my cheeks and the soft firmness of the hand that wipes them. You are my very breath, the breath, even, that comes with the gasp of a sob. You are all and in all. In You I live and move and have my being. You are Home. Here I am.

As I step into my car to drive away from Sister Margaret's for the last time, I see it. There, beneath her front window, is a large pot. In that pot is an oak. The oak sprawls high and wide, reaching above the windowpanes to the top of the first floor. Soon, I know, it will be planted in the ground. I drive away with tears dripping from my chin and pull to the side of the road to catch my breath. I am so grateful. Sister Margaret is Home for me, and look at how I have grown in her presence, in her grace. She has been the mouthpiece of God. As I pull back onto the road, a hawk circles above me, a consecration.

On July 14, I buckle Everett into his car seat and look around our yard one last time. The grass is dry and brown in several places, and the concrete strewn with red bristles from the bottlebrush tree. Paint has chipped from the back of the house and fallen into the overgrown arugula. A hummingbird darts under the clothesline. Everywhere, I see the hand of God.

This is the place of my transformation.

I close the gate.

EPILOGUE

THE FLOOR BENEATH MY FEET
My feet hit the ground
bare, cool wood,
solid.
It feels like home beneath my feet.

IT IS SPRINGTIME. I sit knee-to-knee with three other women on a many-colored Belizean blanket. It is a feast—belated, but in honor of my thirty-first birthday. We laugh freely under the tall trees, but there are also tears.

I spent my birthday traveling across the country with Everett, home from my grandmother's funeral. It was the second of two last-minute trips to the Midwest within two weeks, and my heart aches to be near my family in this time of grief. Each of these other new friends of mine also carries a story of unmet longing; we are each a little heartsick with hopes deferred.[1]

We sit on a blanket in our dresses and we cry for each other. We ask questions. *What does it mean to have hope when all your hopes are dashed? What does it mean to trust God when there are no guarantees?*

As we talk quietly together, I am filled with gratitude. These women are a surprise. I expected it to take years to find soul-friends in this new

---

1 Proverbs 13:12

place, and here I am—loved and cared for and cried with by these women. Already we are shaping each other, tying more threads between our stories, weaving a fabric of love and life between us that I hope will grow stronger and more pliant as the years go by: strong enough for the moments of pain, pliant enough to hold more stories, to weave new lives and dreams together into this fabric we once called community, and which we now call family.

We sit knee-to-knee in the grass as the light fades, until the air grows cold.

Later, our conversation lingers in my mind. What does it mean that God is faithful when there are no guarantees we will get what we want?

The promise is this: Nothing is wasted.[2] If we are willing, if we continue to show up with open hearts, if we offer our pain as a gift, we will be transformed. When we consent to being present to the life we've been given, when we treat ourselves and each other with love and tenderness, we will be made whole, made new. This is only by the power of the God who was also wounded—for by his wounds we are healed.[3]

If you are living in darkness now, of any kind, I am sorry. It is not right. I believe in a God who weeps with you.

I also believe in a God who will redeem it all.

I believe in a God who brings life from death, a resurrection God. I believe in a God who sets the captives free, a God who used my difficult circumstances to free me from shame and fear that shackled my heart. I believe in a God who forged my heart in the fires of pain and sadness and anger and made me better, a God who makes me new every day.

God is making all things new, even us. In our own small, broken-hearted way, we can be part of remaking of the whole world.

Some days I still wake on the edge of despair. Before I open my eyes, I feel shadows of sadness creeping around my heart. This has been a hard month for my family—a month of hospitals, hospice, and mourning, and finding peace even in fear.

What does it look like to live well with my wounds?

Today, it means this: I will rise early, before Everett, and I will read

2   Romans 8:28

3   Isaiah 53:5

and pray a while. It means when I leave the house to write today, I will also bring my watercolors. It means soon I will write a letter to Stephanie.

You don't have to figure everything out. In fact, you don't have to figure anything out. Paint a picture. Write a poem. Listen to the wind in the trees. When you're at a total loss, put a kettle of water on to boil. Find people who will stand in the gap for you, who will hope for you when you can no longer hope and who will pray for you when you can no longer pray.

You are not responsible for your own transformation. You are responsible only to make space for it, to keep showing up to the life you've been given, with eyes and heart open.

Be kind to yourself. Take courage. You are Home.

INVITATIONS TO PRACTICE

ACT: AN INTRODUCTION TO PRACTICE

OPEN THE SOFT MOUTH OF YOUR HEART

by Stephanie Jenkins

open the soft mouth of your heart,
this is the start,
where your story begins

underneath layers of
achievements, errands, demands,
cravings, compulsions, criticisms,
there is——buried deep——a seed,
there is—far below—a hunger

you are quietly waiting to grow
you are far more hungry than you know

so feed that little seed
with Water, Sun, and Spirit
hold it in the dark Earth of your soul
let its roots sink deep and deeper still
feel it spread through you
with its soft tendrils
let it find and form
in every crevice of who you are

then, let it sprout!
let it grow out of the top of your head
let the seed become a sapling,
then, let it become a tree
let your tree grow
let its arms unfurl to kiss the sky
and hold the sun
and dance the rain
and bow to the wind
let it grow!

let the clouds form a crown for you,
set with stars
let birds and squirrels dwell
in your branches
with their song and their scurry

let the leaves
of your spring and summer
go in your fall
and then, in your winter,
wait
hopeful in rest

be this tree
that reaches up and reaches down
whose profound hunger for Life
makes it grow, strong and tall
whose gentle submission to Life
makes it stand, wise and patient
be the tree
whose roots run through you
whose trunk shoots forth
from the crown of your head

be the tree
start by opening
the soft mouth of your heart

ONE EVENING in the darkening fall, I sit down to read a letter from Stephanie. As is often the case, her words ring true—we are on parallel, if disparate, journeys.

"My heart swells with gratitude," she writes. "This is the gift I have been given… I am less afraid of the dark… No one can really enter the darkness unless faith tells her that love is bigger! And I know and believe *Love is bigger!*"

As I sit under the lights of our patio, gratitude swells within me as well. *This is it!* I think. *This is how we know God is faithful.* When I look at my story and at Stephanie's, I am struck by how they are paradoxically similar and different at the same time: Our worlds came together in our unfulfilled desires to have children. A year and a half later, they diverged—I was pregnant; Stephanie was not. Yet we still walked together, still opened our hearts to each other through continued infertility, parenthood, suffering, and transition. In all of this, we have been transformed. We have discovered art, poetry, and nature as pathways to God. We have come through grief to places of openness and presence and a deep-down belief that we are beloved. Our growing empathy has brought each of us deepening relationships.

The dance of our two stories, above all else, speaks of God's faithfulness. We both prayed urgent, desperate prayers. Some were answered, others weren't. Yet, as we relentlessly opened ourselves to love, God took whatever circumstances we were in and used them to shape us. We are both more like Jesus—more whole, more open, more loving, more assured of who we are as God's children—than we were before. God is faithful; here we are, transformed.

So how do we open ourselves to transformation? Our transformation is the work of God, but we get to invite God to transform us. I used to try to become more like Jesus by changing the way I thought, but it didn't work very well. It's much easier to act your way into a new pattern of thought than it is to think your way into a new pattern of action. If you want to change something about yourself or your life, you have to do something to get unstuck.

What is a spiritual practice? I like the word "practice" because it encompasses both traditional spiritual disciplines and innovative ones.

(Often, practices I think are innovative turn out to be rooted in the church historically, and are new only to me.) I also like "practice" because it reminds me that I am learning; practicing is not about getting things right the first time. Practices are tangible and can be simple.

Most of the practices I have developed have begun with a question or a longing. Often, my questions and longings are what God uses to get my attention. They are nudges from the Holy Spirit. I begin with the question or longing and form a simple plan of action: something new I can try to open myself to God's voice and love in a new way, or to live a little differently than my status quo in order to set myself on a new trajectory. After acting on my plan (or sometimes failing at it!) I take time to reflect on what I have noticed.

Begin with the question or the longing. Is there something you've been thinking about a lot lately? A fear, a desire, something you want to walk away from or seek after? Name it: Say it aloud or write it down.

Then, make a plan and act on it. Keep your plan simple. The goal is not to transform yourself but to make space for God to work. Try something new and pay attention to what happens.

- Do you want to be more hospitable? Have someone over to your house for dinner once a week for a month. Keep it simple: different people, same meal—something you're comfortable making. Pay attention to how this changes you.

- Do you want to be more creative? Sign up for an art class. Buy a set of watercolors. Make one sketch in your journal every day, and take notice.

- Do you long for close friends? Write down the names of three people you'd like to know better, and invite them all out for coffee. If any of them say yes, then buy them coffee. Look them in the eye. Ask them good questions. Offer them something you're learning or thinking about or worried about.

- Do you want to slow down, stop being so busy? Schedule an hour a day to rest and do whatever you want. Or an hour a week. Or take a sick day.

- Do you want to be freed from fear? Find a verse or a poem that speaks to you. "Perfect love casts out all fear" will do just fine.

Memorize it. Say it every day—upon waking, as you drive in your car, and every time fear strikes you. Pay attention. What happens in your mind and heart and body as those words become a part of you?

What follows is a guide to many of the practices I developed during the years written about in this book. It was through these practices that God worked in me so strongly, assuring me that I was beloved, borne, and blessed.

- Don't try all of these practices at once. Pick one a week at most and stick with it for a little while. Come back to the others as the seasons of your life change.
- Keep a journal of what practices you try and what you notice as you try them. Where are you resisting? Do you feel God's Spirit nudging you in a particular direction?
- Try a practice with a friend and compare your experiences. What can you learn from each other?
- Stick with each new practice for a little while; sometimes its fruit may take a while to ripen.
- Modify the practices as you see fit, and come up with a few of your own.
- Note the practices that are the most meaningful to you. Out of experiments such as these, you can find a sustained rhythm of practice for your life. (For example, I now take a personal retreat three or four times each year, because they ground me.)

Do one of these things—do anything—and pray. Pray for transformation, or at least for movement or change. Pray that something will be loosened in you. Let go of your desire to control the outcome, and trust that in this tiny (or large) act of faith, God will work and you will never be the same. You may not notice anything at first, but trust that with this tiny shift of your trajectory, your life may become dramatically different in a few years.

Mine did.

PRACTICES FOR
SEASONS OF DISAPPOINTMENT

How do I recognize my belovedness
when I am living with unmet longings?

THE FEELINGS CLOSET (P. 34)

»The Question: How do we create space to experience our emotions?

»The Longing: To know the tender places within us in order to experience God's love more fully.

»The Plan:

1. Pay attention. Are you angry today? Do you find yourself more easily frustrated than usual? Perhaps there is some emotion you're not aware of surging under the surface. Did something happen that brought you to tears? Are you overwhelmed with gratitude or pride in an accomplishment?

2. Pause. Take some time to allow yourself to feel that emotion. If you can, go into a room alone and be still. Dance if you're happy or cry if you're sad. If you are in public, go to your car, or to the bathroom. If you have nothing else to hide behind, cry a little bit behind your sunglasses until you have the chance to be alone. Welcome whatever it is that you are feeling, allow it to course through you, to wash over you like a wave in the ocean, and to recede.

3. Mark this moment. Write a simple poem in your journal. Create a crazy hodge-podge art piece. Copy the words of a Psalm of praise or lament. Throw a rock into the ocean or throw a party.

What it looks like for me:

In the early days of uncovering my depression, my friend Michelle told me that I seem to separate my feelings from my experiences. She said maybe life would be a little easier if I felt things as I experienced them, rather than separating the feeling from the experience.

She's right—for many years, I shoved all of my feelings into a closet in the back of my mind. I tried to label them and categorize them first, but that didn't always work, and mostly I just wanted them out of sight. I stuffed in grief over broken relationships, anger at betrayal, sadness about distance from my family, frustrations at work, all sorts of things—one on top of the other, slamming the closet door shut quickly each time. My feelings closet looked like a high school kid's closet right after his mom made him clean his room—everything jammed in as quickly as possible to hide the mess. This was subconscious work.

Imagine my fear and confusion when, eventually, my feelings closet became full and poured open, spilling out feelings in wave after wave, feelings that were no longer tied to events or experiences but just existed: chaotic, irrepressible, robust. I was overwhelmed and confused. From where did this onslaught come? I cried and cried, often by myself, and sometimes with a very loving, confused, and concerned Dave. Eventually, the cavalcade of grief would pass, replaced by a low, dull feeling of shame at my own weakness and inexplicable grief.

So how do we open ourselves to grief—or joy—in the moments that bring up those feelings? Pay attention, pause, and mark the moment. Markers for me are most often creative: a simple painting or a short poem, or perhaps a collage—sometimes images that are not my own are easier to work with.

I have noticed that sometimes joy is as hard to feel and to mark as sadness. For a while, we had regular "brag time" with our housemates—we shared something that had happened that week that we were excited about or proud of. It could be something big or small—a conversation that went better than expected, an A on a paper, a small act of courage or kindness. In celebrating these stories of success with each other, we marked those moments together, and we spurred each other on to more good deeds.

FIELD TRIPS (P. 38)

»The Question: How do we enjoy ourselves alone with God?

»The Longing: To enjoy ourselves in the presence of God and remember that we are fun.

»The Plan: This week, take yourself on a field trip. Or, as a friend once aptly put it, date yourself. Think about how you would plan an afternoon or an evening with another person, and then plan it just for yourself. Do small things to make it special. The beauty of this is that you don't have to worry about what anyone else would enjoy. The difficulty is figuring out what *you* enjoy.

What it looks like for me:

I first started going on weekly field trips when I was experiencing depression and didn't enjoy myself very much. I didn't know where to begin. I started by going on a walk in a garden and bringing my watercolor set. Sometimes, I take myself out for a cup of tea or to a favorite restaurant for lunch.

Here are some ideas to get you started:

- Take yourself out for your favorite food or drink. Bring a book or magazine to read, or maybe a notebook and a pen or markers.

- Go for a walk in an interesting place. Pop into whatever storefronts grab your attention.

- Look up tourist information for your area. Are there places you've never heard of, or ones you've heard about but have never been to? Pick a museum or other local attraction and spend the afternoon.

- Go for a hike in a beautiful place. Bring a backpack with water and a favorite snack and perhaps a book if you like to read.

- Go to a driving range or get a pedicure.

- Bring a blanket to a park and take a nap or color in a coloring book.

- Go to a movie you've wanted to see.

It's not about finding just the right thing; it's about learning how to have fun with yourself. Resist the urge to feel productive. Invite God into whatever you are doing. Don't try to make it overly spiritual: God dwells within us; everything we do is a spiritual act.

BOUNDARIES (P. 43)

»**The Question:** How do we create healthy boundaries while inviting others into our inner lives?

»**The Longing:** To intentionally cultivate relationships that feel intimate and safe.

»**The Plan:** For one week, pause when someone asks you, "How are you doing?" Make an intentional choice about what to reveal. How much and in what way do you want to invite this person into your life today? Pay attention to how this feels and jot notes in a journal. What patterns do you notice?

What it looks like for me:

As I recovered from a broken friendship, I struggled to find appropriate boundaries. Sometimes I felt cared for when people asked me personal questions. Other times, I felt cornered. For a long time, I felt that I needed to answer every question asked of me not just honestly, but completely. In my mind, honesty required full disclosure. So, I bared my heart too often, too freely, and I got hurt.

Then I put up walls of stone around my heart, trying not to let anyone in. When someone asked "how are you?" I would say "fine," when often I was not at all fine.

So how do we walk the line? How do we let people into our lives while maintaining boundaries?

What helped me most in this was the realization that full disclosure of what I am thinking and feeling is a choice. I have the authority to decide how far to let another person into my heart.

Here are some responses I choose from when someone asks me, "How are you?":

The Dodge: Fine, how are you? Having some follow-up questions ready for the other person will quickly make you a master of The Dodge.

The Open Dodge: Work is really fun these days. I'm really loving my students. How about you? This longer answer invites further conversation and invites your conversation partner to share what is happening in his or her life, without revealing much of what is happening in yours. It is true, and invites conversation, but doesn't reveal the state of your heart.

The Open Dodge with a Nod: I'm doing OK. There are some tough things going on, but work is really fun these days... Like the Open Dodge, this response invites conversation without fully opening your heart. It does, however, nod to the deeper things happening within you, which allows for a more open conversation to happen later on with this person.

Keep It Simple: It's been a rough week, but I'm hanging in there. We're still trying to get pregnant, and it's a long road. Thanks for asking. How about you? This response is more forthcoming, but is not a wide-open invitation for further discussion. If your conversation partner asks follow-up questions, you can choose how openly to answer them.

Full Disclosure: I'm having a really rough week. Dave and I are still struggling with infertility, and I just don't know where God is right now. I'm having a really hard time with friendships with other women, and I don't know what to do about it. I cry a lot. Full Disclosure brings your conversation partner immediately into what is happening within you. This response is best reserved for good friends—for people who you already know have the capacity to listen well and hold your story with you.

The Invitation: I'm having a really rough week. It's a little bit heavy, and we don't need to talk more about it right now, but I'm happy to if you're up for it. Do you have time for a longer conversation, or should we save it for another time? This option directly invites the other person into Full Disclosure, but allows them an out if they're not in a place to listen well. Perhaps they are rushing somewhere else, or perhaps they just don't have the capacity to carry your story well right now. It's OK if they take the out. Find someone else to talk with.

Sometimes I make a choice that leaves me feeling shame afterward—I fear that I've shared too much or not enough. That is OK. I am still OK. You are still OK. And we can make a different choice next time. Healthy boundaries take a long time (a lifetime?) to learn.

HOW TO MAKE A FRIEND (P. 50)

»The Question: How do we make friends?

»The Longing: To experience God's love by moving toward relationships with other people.

»The Plan: Do something fun this week. Play a board game or make fondue or organize a game of kickball. Throw a dance party. Organize a photo scavenger hunt around your city or town. Play cards in a coffee shop. Invite people you know well and at least a few people you don't. Turn off the TV. *Enjoy* yourself, and don't try to make the event into something over-complicated or particularly meaningful. That can come later.

Fun is a great way to begin friendship.

What it looks like for me:

Experiencing God's love requires both moving inward in solitude and moving outward into relationship. One of the most tangible ways we experience God is through other people.

I experience this most naturally in meaningful conversation with trusted friends, but that is only one side of what friendship means. I have to challenge myself to have frivolous fun.

About halfway through my freshman year of college, some friends and I formed the Random Fun Friendship Club—RFFC, for short. We didn't drink, and therefore traditional partying wasn't really our game, but we still wanted to have an eventful social life. We knew a lot of other people who weren't into the party scene either, and so we invited them to join our club.

We used the word "Club" loosely—basically, it was an email list, and whenever any one of us had a crazy idea for something fun, we'd send an email out to the group and see who showed up. We were college freshmen, so we had ideas pretty often.

We played hide-and-seek on Bascom Hill. We played full-contact Spoons in the dorm common room, hiding the spoons across the room behind a barrier of pillows. We had a whipped cream fight, and I learned exactly how hard it is to get out of your hair. We played Midnight Urban Disc Golf (a game we invented that ended for good with a broken street light). We laughed a lot and were creative and we acted like children... or, well, college freshmen.

Good friendships are hard-won. They grow slowly with much water, pruning, sunlight, and time.

Start with low-stakes. Be persistent. Tread carefully. Be open to what unfolds.

CREATIVE WRITING (P. 51)

»The Question: How might we invite God's voice into the processing of our (sometimes incomprehensible) feelings?

»The Longing: To process the incomprehensible without having to figure it out; to experience the love of the Creator in our creativity.

»The Plan: Create something—a poem, a painting, a song, or a sculpture—as a way of allowing God to speak. The easiest place to begin may be writing, because that is a creative act we all engage in every day, even if it's only in text messages or email.

Begin with a warm up. Write one of the following words in the middle of a piece of paper: Love, Courage, Fear, Hope, Despair, or Home. For ten minutes, write or draw whatever comes to you around that word. Ask God to speak through your words or pictures. You may simply draw spirals or write down song lyrics that come to your mind. Try to silence your inner critic and listen for the kinder, quieter presence of God's spirit within you.

Next, spend thirty minutes writing, drawing, composing, or otherwise creating based on one or more of the starters below:

- I/She/He had never before understood
- The rising sun revealed
- Under the darkened moon
- And then I knew
- I am / You are / Together, we are
- When the sky turns black
- Only in the wind

When you are finished, look over what you have created. What do you notice? Does anything surprise you? Is there more you have to create? What did the process feel like to you? Is there anything you want to pray?

What it looks like for me:

In my season of darkness, I needed to find a way to dive deeper into it. I looked for ways to unpack my heartache. God, the creator, speaks to us as we create. Art of all kinds allows us to process something without having to figure it out.

Words are the most natural medium for me, as for many of us, because they are our currency for navigating the world. Though you may not identify as a poet, if other types of art are intimidating for you, begin with writing. You never have to show anyone what you've written.

When writing, sometimes a poem comes out (though they rarely rhyme) and sometimes a paragraph comes out. Sometimes I think it's a paragraph, but it turns out it really is a poem, and it just needs line breaks.

Whatever you create, remember this: Art doesn't have to be beautiful. It just has to represent some kind of truth.

When I write like this, sometimes words and images flow out of me that don't make any sense to me at first glance. Sometimes, it's only later in the rereading that I notice patterns and make some meaning out of them. In the writing of this book, metaphors took on new meaning during the editing process, years after I had written them. Be patient.

PRAYER OF ACCEPTANCE (P. 55)

»The Question: How do we practice acceptance of what God is—and isn't—doing within us?

»The Longing: To let go of responsibility for our own transformation and allow God to work within us.

»The Plan: Find a quiet place for reflection and bring your journal. Take some time to ponder these questions:

- What am I worried about today?
- What am I thankful for?
- Is there anything that I'm frustrated with in my world?
- Is there anything that I'm frustrated with within myself?
- In what area would I most like to grow?

After taking some time to reflect, sit with your hands open before you, and offer up a prayer of acceptance of God's control over your transformation. Then, take a moment to sit in silence and allow God to love you.

What it looks like for me:

As I sought to find God in my season of disappointment, I had to fight my tendency to control my own transformation. I wanted to heal my way on my timeline. I needed to let go.

My prayer was this: *God, grant me the faith of an acorn. May I find life in death and trust that my transformation comes from you. Today, I acknowledge that I feel _____ and I long for _____. I release those things to you. I trust you to love me as I am. I trust that I will grow, like a river awash with rain, without striving.*

Life is a strange balance between bravely chasing after transformation and trusting and accepting that God will transform us when the time is right. I am not sure I will ever figure out the secret to this balancing act. For today, let's take some time to walk in trust and acceptance that the power for transformation is not our power.

Pray with joy, because "he who began a good work in you will carry it on to completion until the day of Christ Jesus."[1]

---

1 Philippians 1:6

HOW TO CRAFT A SPIRITUAL RETREAT (P. 58)

>**The Question:** How do we create space for God to meet us?

>**The Longing:** To carve out time and space for stillness and invite God in.

>**The Plan:** Set aside an overnight, or at least one full day, to spend alone with God. Find a retreat center, use the home of a friend who is away, or head into the woods. Bring whatever might help facilitate your time, but keep it simple. Try to let go of your expectations and just to be present with God.

Some advice:

- Get a good night's sleep the night before.
- Eat a healthy breakfast that will stick with you, but nothing so heavy that you will feel sluggish (think an egg and a smoothie or peanut butter toast and fruit).
- Dress comfortably in layers.
- When you arrive, take some time to know the place. Wander around and look at things; touch them and smell them.
- Silence the other voices—your cell phone for certain. Don't watch the clock.
- Move your body—stretch or go for a walk.
- Rest—take a bath or a nap.
- Don't read much or write much; don't absorb or produce much. If you want to read, read one verse, or maybe a psalm or a poem.
- If you find yourself distracted by things you need to take care of, allow yourself a piece of paper to jot them down so you can put them out of your mind.

Whatever you do with your day, invite God along.

What it looks like for me:

The goal of my personal retreats is to rest and re-center on God. I like to be by myself where I can kneel or sing or cry uninhibited, so I usually find a retreat center or borrow the home of a friend who is at work for the day.

I bring with me:

- my travel watercolor set
- good walking shoes
- lavender oil
- collage materials and paint
- a book of poems
- a blanket and camping chair
- healthy, tasty snacks

You may, like me, be tempted to take a retreat because you need to figure some things out. You need to sift through your emotions, label them, and file them away. You have a few problems you need to solve and make yourself lists of next-steps. You need to plan your calendar for the next nine months. You need to make lists, lots and lots of lists. Resist the temptation. Set no agenda. Do whatever it is you need to do in the moment. This is scary at first, but it gets easier. Trust that you are held in love, that God knows you better than you know yourself. If you feel uncomfortable at any time, call a friend and ask them to pray for you.

If you would like further guidance, try one or more of these stations:

Station 1: Scripture

Take some time to read and meditate on one of these passages of scripture. Consider meditating by journaling, creating a collage, sitting in silence, or taking a walk.

Isaiah 30:15 In return and rest you will be saved; quietness and trust will be your strength.

↳ *Why do we rest?*

Jeremiah 17:5-8
5 This is what the Lord says:
"Cursed is the one who trusts in man,
   who draws strength from mere flesh
   and whose heart turns away from the Lord.
6 That person will be like a bush in the wastelands;
   they will not see prosperity when it comes.
They will dwell in the parched places of the desert,
   in a salt land where no one lives.
7 "But blessed is the one who trusts in the Lord,
   whose confidence is in him.
8 They will be like a tree planted by the water
   that sends out its roots by the stream.
It does not fear when heat comes;
   its leaves are always green.
It has no worries in a year of drought
   and never fails to bear fruit."

↳ *What must you believe, about yourself and about God, in order to rest?*

Matthew 3:16-17 As soon as Jesus was baptized, he went up out of the water. At that moment heaven was opened, and he saw the Spirit of God descending like a dove and alighting on him. And a voice from heaven said, "This is my Son, whom I love; with him I am well pleased."

↳ *What would it look like to let God love you?*

I Kings 19:11-13 The Lord said, "Go out and stand on the mountain in the presence of the Lord, for the Lord is about to pass by." Then a great and powerful wind tore the mountains apart and shattered the rocks before the Lord, but the Lord was not in the wind. After the wind there was an earthquake, but the Lord was not in the earthquake. After the earthquake came a fire, but the Lord was not in the fire. And after the fire came a gentle whisper. When Elijah heard it, he pulled his cloak over his face and went out and stood at the mouth of the cave.

↳   *How do you recognize the voice of God?*

Station 2: Follow a Creature

Go for a walk, then find a place to sit for a while. Choose another created being to observe—an insect, a flower, a rock. Watch it for longer than feels comfortable. What do you notice? What does this being teach you about God, the world, or yourself?

Station 3: Nap

Find a blanket and a quiet spot in the grass. Invite God to rest with you. Imagine God's love covering you like a blanket. Sleep, or don't, but quiet your mind and heart.

Station 4: Create

Choose several collage images that speak to you—don't analyze why. Glue them to a piece of paper, then paint or draw over or around them if you wish. It doesn't have to be beautiful. This is an act of listening and surrendering, of allowing God to use your hands to express some kind of truth. When you finish, take some time to look at your creation—what might God be saying to you in the colors, shapes, pictures, patterns, or chaos?

Station 5: Wander

Go for a wander-walk. Don't try to get anywhere in particular, just see where your feet take you. What do you notice around you? Talk to

God about what you see. Ask God questions, if you have them. Listen for a response, but don't work hard to discern an immediate answer. Perhaps the answer will reveal itself in time.

Station 6: Snack

Fix yourself a snack and perhaps a cup of tea. Eat and drink slowly, savoring the taste. What do you notice in the flavors? What do these foods make you feel? What do they reveal to you about God?

Station 7: Poems

Find a poem that strikes you. Copy it slowly, word by word. What does it reveal? What words stand out to you? If you like, play around with writing a similar poem of your own—but stop if you find yourself frustrated or trying to create something perfect.

Station 8: Silence

Find a place to sit in silence. You may want to repeat a word or phrase (such as "Jesus," or "Lord Jesus Christ, have mercy on me"), or you may want to focus on a place, like a forest, the edge of a stream, or a rocky beach. Pay attention to words, phrases, or images that come to mind. Let distracting thoughts pass by like boats floating down a river.

COLLAGE PAINTINGS (P. 65)

»The Question: How might I hear God in a new way?

»The Longing: To open ourselves to God's voice as we create.

»The Plan: Create a collage as a way of listening.

1) Read a verse or a poem, or say a prayer inviting God to speak with you in your art. Take a few slow, deep breaths to center yourself.

2) Start with a small canvas or a piece of paper (4x6 is just fine). Choose a few images from old books or magazines that speak to you somehow, then glue them to your canvas. Use lots of glue, layering it under and over the pictures, and wiping them flat with a rag or a sponge or your finger.

3) Take out some paint—craft paint will work, though even cheap acrylic paint covers the canvas a bit better, which can be nice for collage. You do not have to wait for the glue to dry. Paint around, or even over, the pictures, with lines or splotches or swirls of color. If you keep a rag handy, you can wipe some of the paint off of the pictures and let them show through. Sometimes I add my own designs to the pictures, like white dots lining the edge of a butterfly wing. Experiment with painting with different materials— sponges or old credit cards. I like using a brayer, which is like a tiny paint roller. Use whatever colors and patterns strike you—it doesn't have to be a picture of anything in particular. If you end up completely covering your collage pictures, that's OK. You can also add more layers of collage on top of the paint—maybe a word or phrase that stands out to you.

4) When you finish, look back over your work and reflect. Don't try to determine whether it's "good" or "bad"—those categories are irrelevant here. Instead, reflect on what truth your art is speaking. What might the pictures and colors you chose represent? Does the art reveal some truth about what you are experiencing right now? Does it bring up any questions within you? How did you feel as you created it?

5) Consider inviting a trusted friend or two to look at the piece and share with you what they see. Sometimes a second pair of eyes reveals new truth.

What this looks like for me:

As I learned to listen for God's love in my disappointment, I found art an effective tool. Art helps me shut down my inner dialogue because it keeps my hands busy.

When I collage, I have to remind myself not to think too much about which images to choose. Sometimes I have a hard time turning off the analytical part of my brain, but that's exactly why this way of listening is good for me. When I look back at collages I made years ago, sometimes a new layer of meaning will unfold.

Art can be scary. When I was a teacher, students often told me, "I can't draw." Now, as I lead adults through spiritual practices, they often say, "I'm not an artist." I didn't identify myself as an artist until just a few years ago, but we are all artists, of some kind— we are all meaning-makers, putting physical form to abstract truth through the way we live our lives.

Art is not about beauty; it is about truth-telling. What you create doesn't have to be beautiful. I hope you discover a new way to hear and express truth.

Art doesn't have to be your "thing." Art is my thing, along with writing, and it may not be yours. Your thing could be running or cooking or public speaking. There are as many different ways to talk to God as there are ways to be human. Find one that works for you, and chase after it. Be willing to try other people's ways to talk with God as well.

HOW TO BLESS A FRIEND (P. 79)

»The Question: What does it look like to bless a friend?

»The Longing: To experience God's love more fully by sharing it with another.

»The Plan: Pray a blessing over a friend who might need it. Keep your eyes and ears open for opportunities to bless those around you with your words.

What this looks like for me:

When I was ready to give birth, I was blessed by my dear friend still in the throes of her infertility. Blessing another person is a way to be present together in our sorrows and our joys.

Blessing someone is new to me. It feels strange, like I shouldn't have that power. It *is* powerful, not because I am powerful, but because God is powerful.

I begin by asking permission to bless my friend. I often rest my hands lightly on his or her shoulders, or one on their forehead.

I usually begin with the lines from Numbers: "May the LORD bless you and keep you..." Sometimes I continue with the well-loved words of those verses (below), or I improvise, like I do in prayer:

May God grant you faith, freedom from fear, and the courage to take the next step.

May God free you from all shame and bless you with security in your identity as a beloved child.

May God take care of your physical needs and bless you with strength and perseverance when what you have seems like it is not enough.

You may be surprised by the words that come from your mouth, or you may not even remember exactly what they were afterward. Or you may write down your blessing and read it word-for-word. Either way, trust that it is what it is called—a *blessing*, a good gift to the receiver.

"The Lord bless you
  and keep you;
the Lord make his face shine on you
  and be gracious to you;
the Lord turn his face toward you
  and give you peace."[2]

---

2 Numbers 6:24-26

PRACTICES FOR
SEASONS OF DISILLUSION

*How do I know that I am borne by God
when my life and self are not what I thought they would be?*

DAILY ART (P. 85)

>**The Question:** How can I connect with God as my identity is shifting?

>**The Longing:** To connect with God daily; to remember my identity as a beloved daughter.

>**The Plan:** We are made in the image of God, the Creator. In seasons of disillusion, when we are wondering who we are, creativity can help ground us in God's love. Find one simple creative project you can do every day for at least a week:

- write a haiku
- paint a watercolor
- sketch a piece of fruit or a flower as it blooms

How do you find yourself looking at the world differently because of this practice?

Invite a friend to try it with you, and share your work with each other. Do it without judgment—either of their art or your own. Simply let each other know what you notice, and encourage each other's efforts.

What this looks like for me:

In the summer of my pregnancy, trapped on the couch, I struggled to remember that I was God's beloved daughter. I needed a new creative practice; I didn't feel like writing. For my birthday, my mom had given me a notebook of watercolor paper and a travel set of watercolors, so I put them to use.

Each day, I read a poem. That summer I favored Wendell Berry and Mary Oliver. I chose a line or two that stood out to me, and I wrote them somewhere on a small watercolor page in permanent ink. Then I painted over and around those words, illustrating whatever stood out to me.

I liked some paintings better than others, but that didn't really matter. I had never used watercolor before, so I learned about the medium by experimenting with it. Most importantly, I sat in God's presence and remembered that I am a created, creative being.

FIGHT FOR REST (P. 99)

»**The Question:** How do we rest in seasons when it feels impossible?

»**The Longing:** To rest in our identity as God's beloved children.

»**The Plan:** Set aside time to intentionally rest. Choose an activity that feels restful to you: going for a walk, reading a novel, listening to music, or taking a nap. Rest for at least fifteen minutes each day or for two hours once a week.

»**What this looks like for me:**
The tasks of motherhood dominated every minute when my son was born. It felt impossible to find time for myself. Rest seems like something we should be able to do in the margins of our days: When we finish up everything else we have to do, and before the next thing comes along, we can rest. But that will never happen. Never will I finish my to-do list. When Everett was tiny, Dave watched him for at least two hours every weekend so I could get away. I went out for coffee or sat in a park, reading or journaling or painting. For me, true rest requires time away from screens. I crash in exhaustion in front of a TV show, but I don't rest.

You have to fight for rest. You will never rest accidentally. You may distract or entertain, but rest requires intention. You have to decide it's worth fighting for.

Make the time because it's worth it for you and for everyone else in your life. I am kinder when I'm not operating on empty. I don't always come home from my hours away happy, joy-filled, and tranquil, but those hours fill me up for later. They make me more willing to give time to someone else. Funnily enough, they make me crave *more* time alone, and I'm more likely to spend Everett's naps reading and reflecting and praying and creating instead of scurrying and checking Instagram.

I want to live as if time is abundant—to give it freely, without fear of scarcity. It *is* abundant, isn't it, if we believe in eternity? The best way I've found to share time freely is to guard just a little bit for myself—time that helps me attune to the voice of the Spirit and rest in my identity as beloved.

SHHHHHHHHH.... (P. 105)

>**The Question:** How do we listen for the voice of God?

>**The Longing:** To still our minds and attune ourselves to God's voice.

>**The Plan:** For a set amount of time each day, listen in silence for God.

What this looks like for me:

In my moments of desperation after Everett's first surgery, I began to listen intentionally for the voice of God. I started with six minutes each day. I often kneel, either on the floor of our bedroom or on our porch outside.

Finding time feels impossible these days. I have to set aside the first six minutes when my son is down for his nap, or I will miss my window.

Sometimes I light a candle to begin—a reminder of the power of the Holy Spirit, the Light of God living in me. I set a timer so I don't have to think about how long I'm spending.

I sit or I kneel, and some days when my mind is racing so fast that I can't calm it, I stand, arms open, like on the edge of a precipice. I ask God to speak, to be present with me. Then I listen.

My mind races. Sister Margaret says that when thoughts come, you can just watch them sail past like boats along a river. Don't analyze or judge, just let them go. I come back to a word or a phrase: *Jesus,* or *Lord Jesus Christ, have mercy on me,* or *walk with me.* Or I center myself around a place, real or imagined, where I can sit with God. Or I come back simply to my breath.

I wait.

Sometimes, something comes to me—a word or a phrase or an image. Sometimes it makes sense, and sometimes it doesn't, and either way I write it down—new layers of meaning might reveal themselves later. Sometimes nothing comes to me, and that is OK, too. Opening myself to listening tunes my ears to the frequency of God. I see God moving throughout my world more easily after those times.

DRAW YOUR FEELINGS (P. 109)

»**The Question:** How do we process feelings we don't understand?

»**The Longing:** To creatively process feelings that can't be sorted out rationally; to connect with God and our own selves.

»**The Plan:** Find a way to creatively represent your feelings. You could play an instrument, draw, or dance. Express the inexpressible through art. Ask yourself, *what does my heart look like today?* Don't think about what you should create, just begin. Try closing your eyes. Don't be surprised if it feels funny and you don't really understand what you've created. That's OK. You probably don't really understand what is in your heart, either, and that's OK, too. Art helps us express what is happening inside of us, when words don't suffice. Offer your art as a prayer.

What this looks like for me:

When I was struggling with guilt over Everett's surgery, I couldn't explain my feelings. I needed to draw them. I often didn't use shapes or forms, just colors, patterns, and scribbles. My drawings were usually a bit of a mess, but I felt lighter after making them.

HOW TO MAKE A FRIEND 2.0 (P. 113)

»**The Question:** How do we deepen friendships?

»**The Longing:** To experience God's sustaining love through deepening friendships.

»**The Plan:** Take some intentional steps toward friends in order to deepen your relationships. If you are not sure where to begin, try an idea from the list below. Take the time to reflect afterward. How did the intentionality feel? What are your hopes for the friendship? Have you communicated them?

What this looks like for me:

There are certainly circumstances that cause friendships to deepen, particularly going through something difficult together. But how do we cultivate deep friendships in the everyday? When I was struggling to feel God's sustaining love even in hard circumstances, I created a book/cooking club with a small group of women. Through those deepening relationships, I discovered some practical steps toward healthy and affirming friendships.

- Say "I love you" out loud. When you find yourself thinking of a friend, send her or him an encouraging text message. Take the time to tell your friends that you appreciate them; it cultivates trust. How many of us walk away from an especially vulnerable conversation wondering what the other person is thinking? Telling each other what we're thinking takes away anxiety.
- Invite people into your life. Friends rarely just keep showing up on your doorstep; you have to invite them. (What if you want to spend more time with someone than they want to spend with you, or vice versa? Different people have different capacities for friendship, and it's important to talk about your hopes and expectations. Inevitably, you will disappoint one another. If you want

to deepen or sustain a relationship, but can't meet their expectations, ask yourself, "How *can* I love this person? What do I have the capacity for?")

- Allow other people to meet your needs. Asking for help is countercultural, and it requires vulnerability. Letting people know your needs allows them into your life in a deeper way.

- Meet someone else's needs. Pay attention to the needs of the people around you and fulfill them, unasked.

- Offer your heart first. If you keep waiting for vulnerability to just happen, it may never come. Begin by offering something personal, but not your most tender hurts or hopes, and see how it is received. Again, different people have different capacities for depth, and that is OK. The more secure you are in your own belovedness, the better you'll be able to weather indifference or even rejection.

- Ask good questions. Sometimes people want to share their stories, but they are just waiting for an opening. Listen well. Ask questions and follow-up questions. Receive whatever it is the other person offers of themselves with openness, grace, and encouragement. Remember, deep friendships happen when people feel safe. Do your best to hold your friend's story in love and patience. Instead of offering advice, simply reflect back to your friend what you hear.

- Celebrate and grieve together over the long haul. This is one of the hardest things. Inevitably in a long-term friendship, one of you will be grieving while the other is celebrating. In order to stay close during those seasons, you have to hold yourself open to one thing while you're immersed in another. That can be painful, and it requires great courage. Sit with someone in their pain—or their joy—longer than feels comfortable.

- Say you're sorry. This is one I'm working on. I'm not very good at "sorry"— I'm better at either rationalizing any error I've made or catastrophizing about what a horrible person I am, neither of which is helpful. Give grace to each other and yourself.

WHISPERS (P. 118)

»The Question: How do we tune our ears to the voice of God?

»The Longing: To learn to recognize God's voice.

»The Plan:

I wish there were a straightforward plan for revelation. If there is, I haven't found it yet. Most often, revelations come as a surprise; our work is to prepare ourselves to recognize them when they come. That preparation is multifaceted. It requires regularly turning our minds and hearts to God.

Take a few minutes each day, for at least a week, to write down something that God might be saying to you. What do you notice as you go about your days? What conversations, songs, words you read, or images you see stay with you? Look back over your notes and watch for convergence.

What this looks like for me:

I have heard from God most clearly in the times in my life when I've persisted in a regular rhythm of practices. For me, that means time each day either in silence, prayer, art, or journaling. It means longer periods of time every week or so reading and creating. It means even longer periods of time every few months when I get away for a day to be with God. It also means maintaining close friendships with people who talk with me about God and how they are learning and growing.

How do we recognize the voice of God? I have not found a simple answer to that question, but I've asked a lot of people, and here are some of the things they've said:

- The voice of God is quiet, but persistent. It requires attention.
- The voice of God is gentle, kind, and loving.

- The words of God align with what we know to be true about God from the Bible.
- Convergence: God often tells us the same thing in many ways: books, songs, the voices of friends, even dreams. God speaks in the synchronicity of images and words and feelings and thoughts and circumstances all coming together to point in one direction.
- Familiarity: The more time you spend listening, the easier it becomes to recognize the voice of God. You develop a language together, like inside jokes with a good friend.

Sometimes I worry about whether I am hearing from God or just thinking or imagining something. How can I tell God's voice from my own? But maybe it doesn't matter whether or not the word or image you receive is "really from God." Maybe, if the things you're telling yourself are kind, loving, true, and full of grace, those things are coming from the Spirit of God living in you.

LAYING DOWN OUR BURDENS (P. 124)

»**The Question:** How do we let go of the things that weigh upon us?

»**The Longing:** To let go of the things that weigh us down and experience God's sustaining love.

»**The Plan:**

What are you carrying around with you these days? Are you holding onto feelings of responsibility for something out of your control? Are you longing for freedom from a past mistake or a past hurt? Do you feel pressure, perhaps, to carry the weight of another person's happiness?

Start by naming the thing that weighs on you. Write it down. Find someone you trust, and say it aloud—secrets lose their power over us when they are brought to light.

Then ask yourself this question: Do I have work left to do here? Before you are freed from this burden, is there anything you need to do to be released? Is there a step you need to take toward reconciliation or healing? Perhaps there is a conversation that needs to be had or an apology that needs to be made.

Then put a rock in your pocket. Find one next time you are outside somewhere. It can be rough or smooth, many colored or plain gray, but should have enough weight to it to feel it there in your pocket.

Carry it around for a while—maybe a day or two, or maybe a week. Let that rock come to represent this burden you've been carrying. Perhaps, if you do still have work left to do, this rock can be a reminder to take courage—the hard work is worth it. Take it out and look at it once in a while, when you find yourself thinking of this burden you're carrying, or just stick your hand in your pocket and feel its edge, and pray.

Pray for courage. Pray for the wisdom to know how to let go and the courage to do so. Pray for forgiveness or for the ability to forgive.

When you are ready, let go. Give up that rock in your pocket. Throw it into a body of water if you have one handy, or even just into the public garbage can outside the grocery store. Pray for release. Claim release. Every day after, continue to claim it, "for my yoke is easy, and my burden is light."[1]

What this looks like for me:

For many months, I carried around guilt over my son's surgeries, because on a primal level I believed it was my responsibility to protect him from all harm. In order to allow God to carry me, I had to let go of that lie.

I tend to carry more responsibility for the lives of others than I should. I also carry guilt and shame around for a long time when I have made a mistake. "Sorry" doesn't come as easily to me as "but I..." or "but you..." It helps me immensely to remember that the God who began my transformation for good will carry it on to completion.[2]

1　Matthew 11:30
2　Philippians 1:6

THE FEELINGS CLOSET, REPRISE (P. 130)

»**The Question:** What does it look like to lament?

»**The Longing:** To express our anger and sadness to the God who is big enough to handle it.

»**The Plan:** The next time your eyes unexpectedly well up with tears, make time and space for them to fall. Go to your room, your car, the bathroom—anywhere you can, as soon as you can. Cry. Yell or silently scream; tell God all the things that have gone wrong and all the ways you're undone by what is happening in your life or in the world, and ask *why, why, WHY?!* as many times as you need to. Do it for a minute or ten or ninety and don't be afraid the grief will consume you. It doesn't have that power. Let it wash over you, tumble you to the ground, spin you and rock you till you're not sure which way is up. And then let it roll away. It will not be finished— these things don't have an end—but you can let some of the pressure out. When we grieve, we make space for new things to take root in us, and the waves of grief water our souls.

Sometime after, make time to reflect. Write about what you've experienced and what you're feeling. Write with feeling; use language of extremes. If you don't have words, use someone else's until you do. Copy a lament from the Bible and make its words your own. Try Ecclesiastes 3, Psalm 13, Psalm 22, Psalm 44, Isaiah 58, Matthew 23:37-39, or Matthew 27:46.

What this looks like for me:

For me, lament is private, and therefore easy to avoid by filling my days with people and books and errands and chores. I am learning that I don't function well that way; things build up and overwhelm or "come out sideways," as a friend of mine says—in anger or frustration with those closest to me. When I create space for lament, living each day in joy and gratitude becomes easier.

After my son's surgeries, I learned that one good cry doesn't usually take care of things. I had to open myself, again and again, to the tender places within me. It is frightening at first to plumb those depths, but the more time I spend there, the less I am afraid. I am more and more confident that, by God's help, I will find my way back to the surface.

There are three things I want us to remember:

1. There is no quick or easy answer to grief. When something hard happens, even when it's over, even if everything turns out OK and especially if it doesn't, grief continues to surprise us. A song, a flower, a smell—any of these things can bring it all back. (For me, it's fluorescent lighting, all too reminiscent of the emergency room.) We have to hold ourselves open to grief, hearts splayed wide, before we can keep moving.

2. Lament is an act of worship, an act that allows us to respond to the fullness of who God is: a God who mourns for our hurts and for the injustices in this world.

3. We do not cast our lament into a hopeless void, but into the open arms of our loving God who hears us and who is near. Our God created all things and dwells within each of us; our God is big enough to handle all fear, all rage, and all sorrow. Our God laments for us and with us. We need not be afraid.

CULTIVATE GRATITUDE (P. 131)

»The Question: How do we grow our awareness of the goodness in our lives?

»The Longing: To cultivate gratitude even when circumstances are difficult.

»The Plan:

Every evening or morning, write down a few things you are thankful for. Do it someplace convenient: a journal next to your bed or a note on your phone. Pay attention to the kinds of things for which you are thankful. What in your life brings you joy?

If you are feeling insecure about who you are, include at least one item on your list about yourself—something about the way God made you for which you are grateful.

Take it to another level by saying your thanks aloud. If you find yourself thankful for a friend or a family member, tell them so. When someone asks you how you are doing, tell them some of the things you are thankful for that day.

Practicing gratitude forces you to pay attention. Cultivate your gratitude and watch how it grows.

What this looks like for me:

The first year of my son's life was difficult for me. I wrestled with my identity as a mother, as well as sleep deprivation and out-of-whack hormones and the hard reality of his surgeries.

Stephanie mentioned that she was having her students make a gratitude list each day, and it sounded like a good idea. I started a note on my phone, and each day before bed I wrote down three to five things for which I was grateful.

Often, they were very simple: a good nap for Everett, lemons from the tree in our front yard, lavender-scented soap, or a quiet moment alone with Dave. The act of writing them down adjusted my sight each day. I saw my world, at least sometimes, through the lens of gratitude. Life will not always be easy, but there will always be moments of goodness if we pay attention.

EMBRACING SEASONS (P. 133)

>**The Question:** How do we live into the season in which we find ourselves?

>**The Longing:** To recognize the season we are in and embrace it.

>**The Plan:**

What season are you in right now? Are you experiencing the release of autumn? The dormancy and waiting of winter? The new life of spring or the fullness of summer?

Choose the season that you most identify with at this moment, and think about it for a while. What are the sights, sounds, smells, textures, and tastes that remind you of that season? Summer instantly makes me think of the smell of wet pavement on a hot day. Autumn is all about flavor—pumpkin and squash and cider and spices. Winter is the crackly feeling in my nose when it's so cold out that my nose hairs freeze. And spring, to me, is snowdrops poking through the melting snow.

Make a list of all of these details. Come up with as many as you can. Think of your childhood—sometimes that's easier, because we were more in tune with small things.

Take your list, and create something based on it. Draw a picture, make a collage, write a poem, or compose a piece of music.

Then set it aside for a little while. When you come back to it, look at it without critique. Don't ask yourself "is this any good?" Instead, ask yourself what you can learn from it. How does this piece of art represent what you are experiencing in this stage of your life right now? Are there any elements that stand out? Why do you think that is? What might it look like to live more fully into this season?

Share your work with a friend. Ask them what they see in it, especially if they know you well. You never know what you might discover.

What this looks like for me:

As Everett's second surgery approached, I needed to release my control over his life. Embracing the season of autumn helped me to do so.

My art of choice is often poetry. To turn my list about a season into a poem, I might create a metaphor by beginning each phrase with "I am…" In a season of summer, my poem might begin like this:

> *I am summer.*
> *I am the smell of wet pavement*
> *on a hot day.*
> *I am the ripest strawberry.*

Once, I turned the list into a metaphor for God to create the poem *I Am Winter* (p. 41). This helped me remember the good things in a hard season.

Naming the fact that I am in a season of autumn or winter helps me recognize that there will be an end to it. I may be in a long season, but that season will end. I can hold on to the hope of spring while learning to live well in autumn.

REFLECTIONS ON TRUST (P. 138)

»The Question: What does trusting God look like when everything falls apart?

»The Longing: To relentlessly cry out to God for help, even when we're not sure help will come.

»The Plan:

If you are in a hard situation, this practice is for you. Just keep crying out for help. Sometimes life is so hard it feels impossible to pray. It feels impossible to trust that God will hear and act. It seems to me, in the moments when we most need it, trust is very simple: Just keep crying out for help.

Where do you need help? What would it look like for you to keep crying out?

What this looks like for me:

The aftermath of Everett's second surgery rocked me to my core. I was desperate and angry with God, and I wanted God to fix the situation. I wanted to trust God, but I couldn't begin to imagine what that looked like when I had no guarantees that my prayers would be answered.

What is trust? You don't have to wrestle your heart into some kind of transcendent peace, though that is a lovely gift when you are given it. You don't have to believe without a doubt that everything will be OK, because it may not be—at least in any recognizable sense.

Just keep calling out for help. For me, this means tears of rage. Even when you're not sure help will come, even when you're not sure anyone is listening, even when you're so angry over what is happening to you and the people you love that your call for help becomes a scream of rage: *HELP US! Because you can and you should and you said you would but I CAN'T SEE YOU and I'm not sure I believe you right now, HELP US!*

Maybe that is trust enough, and trust of the most acute variety—a cry of desperation when everything you have is not enough.

PRACTICES FOR
SEASONS OF HOPE

*How do I recognize the blessings I've been
given even as I hope for something new?*

BEAUTY WALK (P. 145)

»The Question: How do we cultivate an awareness of the beauty around us?

»The Longing: To train our eyes to see the beauty before us even when we hope for something different.

»The Plan:

Go for a walk in your neighborhood. You can either wander where your feet take you or walk a route you take often, but with different eyes. As you walk, watch for signs of beauty—bits of green, a smile from someone you pass, a gesture of kindness between a couple walking together. Note these things somehow. You can jot notes in a notebook or on your phone or take pictures as you go.

The purpose of this walk is to look for beauty, but that doesn't mean you have to ignore the ugliness and pain. Mark how those things highlight the beauty.

Walk without listening to music or talking on the phone. Keep all of your senses open to what is happening around you. Does the smell of fresh-baked bread mingle with the car exhaust? Is there music flowing from a neighbor's window?

When you get home, create something tangible that represents the beauty you noticed. Here are a few ideas:

• Write a poem that lists the things you see. You may want to try repeating a phrase or two throughout (sometimes that helps a list-poem feel more poem-like). You could try a phrase like "beauty endures" or "hope grows."

• Create an art piece that represents one (or more) of the things you noticed. It could be a painting, or you could print one of the pictures you took.

- Create a beauty map. Draw a simple map of the route you walked and label important places. Then add symbols or words for the signs of beauty you noticed.

When you are finished with your art, look at it and reflect. What do you notice? How does the contrast of beauty and pain you see in your neighborhood mirror your own heart?

What this looks like for me:

For five years, I waited for God to release us from Los Angeles. I loved our life, but I hoped for a different one: one in Wisconsin with our family. I had to intentionally cultivate my love for our neighborhood, to grow deep roots even though I knew one day we'd tear them up. So I walked, and looked for beauty. Eventually, I found places that I knew brought me joy to visit, and we walked to them several times a week. Barnsdall Park, the taco shop (HomeState), and the neighborhood Goodwill were my favorites.

Looking for beauty helps us remember that life is complex, full of good and bad intertwined. We can see the good even in seasons of darkness when we train our eyes to see.

THRESHOLDS (P. 150)

The Question: How do we invite God into the threshold spaces in our lives?

The Longing: To live well in seasons of waiting by rooting where we are and hoping for what's next at the same time.

The Plan: Are there areas in your life where you feel like you're standing at a threshold? Maybe you are anticipating a change at your job, or a change in the nature of a relationship. Perhaps the way forward is clear, or perhaps it is muddled.

What does it feel like to be in this threshold space? Does it make you uncomfortable, or are you excited by the unknown? Are you looking forward to the impending change or are you dreading it?

What does it look like to live well in a threshold space? It doesn't work well to stand indefinitely on one foot, looking for a place to set down the other. I'd rather live with feet firmly planted. So what does it look like to live with feet planted on one side of a change and eyes turned forward through the doorway?

Brainstorm a list of practices that would allow you to do that. Perhaps you could make a two-column list, one with "feet planted practices" that continue to root you where you are and the other with "eyes forward practices" that help you keep looking ahead. A rooting practice might be spending time weekly with the people who ground you, the people you love in the place where you are. A forward practice might be praying a daily prayer of surrender about what is next.

After you brainstorm, choose one practice from each column to commit to this week. Take notice of what these practices bring up for you.

What this looks like for me:

Sometimes I wonder if life will ever feel settled. All life is a threshold. At least in my experience, we perpetually live in some kind of in-between. Until you find contentment where you are, you will never find contentment anywhere. I have found that the best changes come when I am faithful to the life I'm living. While I was waiting to leave Los Angeles, I resisted the tendency to prematurely distance myself from friends, unless they asked for that distance. I hunted for places that I loved and visited them often. I did these things in spite of the fact that they would make it harder when the time came to leave. I also prayed a lot about our future. I asked God for what I wanted—to move home to Wisconsin—and for what I really wanted, to find a place where our family's life could be more integrated and we could put down deep roots. When my desires overwhelm, I pray this: *your kingdom come, your will be done.*[1]

Cultivate contentment, and keep your eyes on the road ahead.

---

1 Matthew 6:10

LEAVING WELL (P. 160)

»The Question: How do we end a season well?

»The Longing: To recognize the blessings we've been given in order to move into a new season well.

»The Plan: If you are in a season of ending, ask yourself the question, "What would it look like to end this well?" It is not easy to end well. It is a lot easier to cut your losses and run, but saying goodbye is worth the effort.

If the season you are in is ending, take time to intentionally say goodbye. Write letters, visit favorite places, give small gifts to the people who matter to you. Even if all you need is a private ceremony of some kind—one last cup of tea at your favorite table in your old office, accompanied by a prayer of thanks—don't just disappear. Say goodbye as completely as you know how.

What this looks like for me:

When we were leaving Los Angeles, I told a friend of mine that I was soaking in every minute of our time left. She advised I add some "bath salts" to the soak to make it more enjoyable. For me, that meant eating a lot—I visited all of my favorite Los Angeles restaurants one last time. It also meant spending time with the people I loved. And it meant saying "yes" when our friends wanted to throw us a goodbye party on the night before we left.

Two years earlier, when I made the decision to stay home full-time with Everett, I had already been away from school on maternity leave for most of the school year. When I left in June, I thought I would be back in August, but early contractions prevented me from going back to school. Then, I just never went back, except to clean out my classroom. It felt like a strange way to end such a significant period of my life. It wasn't enough.

So I wrote cards. I bought a pack of simple blank note cards, and I wrote cards to all of my coworkers—about fifty. I thanked them for working with me over the years, and for the wisdom and kindness they had shared. It took a long time. I did it for them, but mostly I did it for me; I needed some closure for these relationships that had been such a daily part of my life for six years.

Saying goodbye well is a key part of recognizing the blessings in a season of hope. Our endings color our memories. By saying goodbye with intention, I solidified the positive elements of those seasons of life that I wanted to remember.

A BLESSING AS YOU CLOSE THIS BOOK

Dear reader,

As you walk the road of transformation
may the God who made you,
the God who loves you,
continue to hold you
as I know God will.

May you know the grace and goodness
of this loving God
deep in your bones.

In all of your disappointment,
may you know that you are beloved.
In your disillusion,
that you are borne.
In your hope,
blessed.

May you find a good way through
a way that winds and wanders
under sun and moon, both.

May you know that you are held, close
to the beating of God's own heart.

Peace be with you.

Amen.

ACKNOWLEDGMENTS

THIS BOOK BEGAN when I woke at four o'clock one morning with the certainty that I had lived a story I needed to write. I had come through darkness and found a good path—not a way out, but a way through—and I wanted to help other people find their own way.

The task felt impossible. How, as a stay-at-home parent of a toddler, would I find time to write? I had never successfully kept up a blog, let alone written a book. I nearly dismissed the idea entirely. But...

But I am married to an Ideas Guy. Dave, without you I never would have begun.

But I am surrounded by generous friends who love my children. To the many of you who cared for them so I could write, I am deeply grateful.

But I lived in Hollywood, a place full of brilliant, talented, and creative people. If this book and the things that flow from it are polished, deep, soulful, helpful, or beautiful, it is because I have gifted and generous friends. They encouraged and supported me from the very beginning. When I asked "how?" they said, "like this!" and showed me the way. Cory Howard, you convinced me this was possible that night in the living room of the Big House, and then you made it possible by putting together the perfect Kickstarter video (with the help of Trey Burns and Claire Wellin). I am deeply grateful for the whole Kickstarter team that believed in this project even before I did, especially Rick and Nancy, Seth and Nikki, (Great) Grandpa George, Rick K., Ryan D., Stephanie, Steve and Anne, Shalen and Bethany, Amy and David, Abby, Maya and Mary, Anna, Rebekah and Bob, Joey and Katie, Ryan and Nora, and Matthew. Your generosity gave me a few precious hours each week to write. Because of you, I discovered a passion and vocation I'd never imagined. This book exists because of you.

Thank you to Brianna and all the staff at HomeState—your counter was my office, your lattes my fuel.

Thank you to all of my early readers, especially Katie, Diane, Jessica, Caitlyn, Nikki, Lisa, Erin, Leah, and Nancy. You encouraged and advised me when the manuscript was a newborn—flailing and uncertain, vulnerable and soft. Thank you for helping it mature.

I am grateful for Mark Nepper and Caroline Willis for teaching me to write all those years ago and for those who broadened my vision for what this book could become, especially Jer Swigart, Adrianna Wright, and Andrew Bronson.

Our Kairos and Open Door families—thank you for your friendship, patience, love, and creativity. Thank you for learning to walk in the way of Jesus with me.

Ryan Littrell, you are a skilled designer, a gifted artist, and a great friend. Thank you for making the cover a piece of art. Ben and Myles at BX Films, I am so grateful for your time and talents.

Mark and Lisa Scandrette, you have informed this book in many ways, primarily because you have influenced my life. Thank you for your friendship, for your writing, and for living well.

Paul, you held me to a higher standard then I held myself. You are wise and insightful, always gentle but never indulgent. You took the rough-hewn manuscript, handed me the fine tools of the carver, and taught me to use them. I am a better writer because of our work together.

Nikki, you are my best encourager and fan. Were we not sisters, I would still forever call you friend. Seth, I'm glad to call you family; thank you for loving my sister well.

Mom, your life and vocation inspire countless women to live into their own callings whole-heartedly and bravely, your daughters among them.

Dad, you gave me my love of words all those evenings reading aloud by the fireplace. Thank you for sharing your care for grammar and the transcendent.

Sister Margaret, in your humble wisdom you have become everyone's favorite character in this story. I think of your words daily. Thank you for loving God and following God's Spirit. I miss you dearly.

Stephanie, thank you for living this story with me. Of all the gifts that came from this dark time, your friendship is one of the most precious. You love well, you feel deeply, you see and speak the truth. I would not have found a good way through had we not walked it together.

Everett and Asher, you challenge, inspire, and delight me daily. My capacity to love increased exponentially when each of you arrived. You make be a better human.

Dave, beloved husband, best of friends—you have been cheerleader, coach, friend, and partner from the day this book began and have played each role with wisdom and grace. Thank you for loving me through both the living and the writing of this story. Thank you for your integrity, hard work, and self-sacrifice. You are the wisest man I know.

God above all, in whom everything holds together, there are no words. Thy kingdom come; thy will be done. I sing in gratitude and joy.

I am your beloved.

Here I am.

CONTINUE THE JOURNEY...

For a free group discussion guide and
additional content, visit **KristenLeighKludt.com**.

Made in the USA
San Bernardino, CA
15 February 2017